Initiation into the Grail Mysteries

Initiation into the Grail Mysteries

Advanced Spiritual Teachings, Practices, and
Empowerments for Esoteric World Service

Grailmaster
And
Bishop Timothy A. Storlie

Writers Club Press
San Jose New York Lincoln Shanghai

Initiation into the Grail Mysteries
Advanced Spiritual Teachings, Practices, and Empowerments for Esoteric
World Service

Writers Club Press
an imprint of iUniverse.com, Inc.

For information address:
iUniverse.com, Inc.
5220 S 16th, Ste. 200
Lincoln, NE 68512
www.iuniverse.com

ISBN: 0-595-17482-5

Printed in the United States of America

Contents

Introduction

THE TAPES, LECTURES, AND COMMENTARIES:

Prolegomenon

Significant new spiritual impulses come into our world through the strivings and invocations of unique men and women who have achieved a close attunement with the invisible guides of humanity known in Hermetic terms as Spiritual Hierarchy. The Temple of the Holy Grail is a new spiritual impulse given in the latter quarter of the twentieth century. It is a mystery school designed to empower spiritually mature women and men with Hierarchical attunement for esoteric world service.

This book, and the supplemental taped lectures available, are a revision and abridgment of the original three Teaching Cycles I gave to probationers for Wesak initiation into the Temple of the Holy Grail. Initially, these comprised twenty-two hours of sequential lectures tape recorded in San Jose, California, from September, 1990, through April, 1991, for the first group of T:.H:.G:. candidates, as well as hundreds of pages of privately published teachings.

From 1990 to 1998, over seven seasons of initiation, nearly one hundred spiritually mature, carefully selected candidates in Britain, Europe, North America, Central and South America, Australia, and Indonesia undertook probationary studies for Wesak initiation into the First Order of the Temple and its unique program of seven potent Self-Empowerments done on lunar and solar cycles. T:.H:.G:. computer-linked initiatic centers were established by Templar Initiate Bishops of the International Federation of Gnostic Bishops in London, Spain, Montreal, and in eight Eastern, Midwestern, and Western states of the United States. In 1995, Bishop Alberto LaCava and his New York area group began the project of translating T∴H∴G∴ materials and tapes into Spanish, which facilitated the addition of many Central and South American probationers and initiates.

During this period, T∴H∴G∴ initiates were ordained to the Diaconate of the Apostolic Succession so that they could be authorized to work with consecrated elements for the theurgical operations of the Liturgy of the Holy Grail, which facilitates Self-Empowerments done on new and full moons. Many of them were advanced in Holy Orders into Priesthood and even into the Episcopate (Bishop) by their mentor Templar Bishops.

In 1998, however, I was guided to establish specific spiritual training for Holy Orders as a program separate from T∴H∴G∴. This is now known as the Home Temple Priesthood, which is given an overview in this book and can be found at **http://www.hometemple.org**. Templar initiates, by virtue of having been screened and accepted for T∴H∴G∴, are also qualified to undertake Home Temple training for Apostolic Priesthood.

At initiation, all First Order members of T∴H∴G∴ are licensed as Subdeacons of the Home Temple, provided with pre-consecrated elements, and taught to celebrate the theurgical Liturgy of the Holy Grail in order to operate the seven Self-Empowerments of the First Order. They may, at their own option, elect to advance in Holy Orders through Diaconate and Priesthood by means of the Home Temple training.

In 1998 I was also guided to offer the probationary materials to the general public by revising them and, in collaboration with Bishop Timothy A. Storlie, publishing and distributing a reorganized version of written and taped teachings through the Internet and spiritual book stores. With this method, the people for whom this impulse was brought into the world will be able to find their way to T∴H∴G∴, study the probationary materials and, if so moved, make application to the Temple for

Wesak initiation. Instead of having to travel to a Templar Bishop for initiation, the accepted candidate will be able to operate his or her own Vigil and Initiation using materials and instruction provided, then to undertake the seven Self-Empowerments of the First Order without necessity of travel.

Thus, Hierarchy has created an initiatic mystery school based not upon secrecy, but accessibility, and not upon hidden geographical centers, but a worldwide virtual platform. T:.H:.G:. is not dependent upon secret adepts, but upon self-empowerment. It is focused not merely upon the spiritual achievements of the past, but upon the coming generation of spiritually gifted individuals who are attuning themselves to Divine Will and Hierarchy. T:.H:.G:. exists to facilitate the empowerment of those spiritually talented individuals who have the potential to contribute wonderful new achievements of soul and spirit for the sake of the New Humanity. It is a tool to be used by such people.

I express my profound appreciation to Bishop Boyer for his invaluable spiritual guidance; to my extremely talented wife and Grail Mother for the powerful new esoteric force she has brought into the Temple; to Bishop Timothy A. Storlie for offering to edit, co-author, publish, and distribute these materials; to Deborah Storlie for her careful editing and suggestions; to Bishop Alberto LaCava, whose New York group has developed into a world-wide center for both English and Spanish speaking initiates in T:.H:.G:. and Martinism; and to all other Templar Bishops who have assisted in the development of the Temple.

The T:H:G:. web site is **http://www.HomeTemple.org/THG.htm**

Grailmaster
April 23, 2000 (Easter Sunday)

CHAPTER ONE
THE GRAIL MYSTERIES

Restoring the Paths of the Graal

Great spiritual teachers have developed many and varied pathways to ascend the Mountain of Divine Self. The spiritual imperative for this age is to expand, upgrade, and universalize these pathways so that they can be useful to the New Humanity. The Temple of the Holy Grail has been established to restore and reframe the sacred *Graal* Paths of the Western initiatic tradition. These encompass the gnosis, teachings, and sacred mysteries of apotheosis—the incarnation of divinity within humanity, and of Divine Reality within the human world.

The Temple of the Holy Grail

The Temple of the Holy Grail is an Initiatic Mystery School for men and women ready to undertake private advanced esoteric probation and occult initiatic training in order to anonymously serve human and planetary evolution.

The sacred technology of the Temple safely promotes mastery of psychic perception, intuition, lucid dream-work, soul-projection, yogic *siddhis*, and all of the powers demonstrated by *Mar Yeshua*, the Master Jesus, that lie dormant in normal human beings.

The Eggregore of the Temple is a protective environment where spirit unfolds in the heart by means of initiation, interior spiritual experience, esoteric practices, sacramental grace, and self-empowerment. Initiatic work is done privately in one's home or sanctuary on lunar and solar cycles. The Initiate receives empowerments for the *Imitatio Christi*—the Imitation or Esoteric Way of the Christ—applying shamanic principles of ancient Apostolic Gnosis that were not preserved in Western institutional religion, but transmitted privately in secret traditions beyond the reach of medieval Inquisitors and heresy hunters.

The Western Initiatic Pathways

The *Graal* or "graded advancements" of the initiatic path, has existed to a greater or lesser degree in all religions and cultures, from the inner training of shamanism to the formal Priestly and other mystery schools of Egyptian, Brahman, Greek, Hebrew and other religious cultures.

Initiatic training was carried forward from ancient roots and transmitted into medieval Britain and continental Europe in several streams of Judeo-Christian and Gnostic religion. Western esoteric spirituality is presented in the Graal Teachings of the Mystery Schools which have been traditionally Gnostic, Kabbalistic, Hermetic, and Pan-Theosophical.

By Gnostic we refer to the wisdom and practices of the ancient Pythagorean, Empedoclean, and other Greek mystery schools. By Hermetic we refer to the high teachings of the Egyptian Priestly cult of Hermes Trimegistus that were perpetuated from the School of Achmim in their Gnostic context through Islamic alchemists and mystics, and during the European Renaissance through Rosicrucian, Freemasonic, Illuminist, Martiniste, and Ultramasonic schools. By Kabbalistic we refer to the European medieval Christian-Hermetic development of Jewish Kabbalah, which derived from pre-Hellenistic Jewish prophetic Merkabah Mysticism, Hekhaloth Mysticism, and the synthesis of Chaldaean and Pythagorean Wisdom Teachings in the Hellenistic Jewish Diaspora.

The Holy Chalice

The *Graal* or Grail is the sacred symbol of esoteric and Gnostic Christianity. In Christian Europe it was allegorized as the vessel used by Master Jesus upon which the Christian Eucharist or Mass was based. In the New Testament, Matthew 26:27-28 and parallels describe how Master Jesus at the Last Supper held up the Passover Kiddush Cup before his disciples and told them, "This is my blood of the New Covenant."

Legend tells of Joseph of Arimathea, who supposedly used this same Vessel to gather the blood of the Master when his crucified body was taken from the cross, much as Isis gathered the remains of the slain Osiris. Whatever the historical facts may be, the archetype of the Holy Chalice of the Christ has become one of the driving symbols of Western esoteric spirituality.

The Sangreal

The Sangreal is the *Sang Real* or "Royal Blood," the alchemical Divine Golden Sacrificial Energy that nurtures evolutionary unfoldment in the physical universe and among beings developing on this plane of existence. It is the power that sanctifies matter, quickening its spiritual vibration and level of refinement. It is the actual substance of Blessing ("blissing, sprinkling with Holy Blood") or Bliss. It is the Philosopher's Stone, Elixir, or Amritha that transforms the lower into the Higher, expands the crystallized or contracted Heart-consciousness, and mediates inspiration, guidance, selfless service, and Divine Love. In the Grail tradition this is known as the *San Greal* or "Holy Grail." It is a variation of the Celtic term *Graal* or "Gradual," meaning the step-by-step advancement into initiatic progress on the infinite Path of Light.

In the Temple of the Holy Grail, First Order Templars are trained in esoteric theurgical operations of shamanic Priesthood. They are authorized to use the Liturgy of the Holy Grail and daily practices of the Blessing Way, benefiting immensely from these works when carried out with fiery, selfless devotion to humanity, the Divine Will, and all beings. The Holy Grail is both a theurgical Sacrament for higher human and planetary Initiation and an invisible alchemical process of transformation transmitted through the ancient Priesthood of Melchizedek.

In the Liturgy, Divine Nectars, Fragrances, and Essences of the *San Greal* are poured out as omnipotent blessing for the spiritual evolution of all beings. In the Temple, the Grail Communion is a physical point of contact between Hierarchy and disciples of all ranks through which divine energies are transmitted. It is an oasis of spiritual refreshment and a bubbling spring of inspiration. The Grail Chalice is filled and the Blessings of Heaven are transmitted at a sacred time and place.

The Path to the Grail

There exist many paths within *the* Path. Each seeker makes his or her own way through the interior labyrinth of the Grail Castle, which is the body or microcosm. This interior Grail Castle has been allegorized as Solomon's Temple, the Deity Mandalas of Tibetan Highest Yoga Tantra, the alchemical vessel, and many other things.

Inside this Castle, the Holy Grail lies hidden within the spiritual heart of each individual. It awaits discovery through heart-felt aspiration, deep study, perennial questioning, prayer, meditation, contemplation, and service.

Torkom Saraydarian writes in *The Flame of the Heart*, "Many of our ancient teachers told us the path to the Most High is found through our heart, that the human heart is the doorway leading to the path reaching all the way to the Great Cosmic heart." Palatine in the *Collected Writings of Duc de Palatine* adds, "Buried within the heart of each one of us, being a fragment of the Whole, is hidden the Lord of Divine Life, and He dwells there to guide, the Guardian which hath shined in our hearts. This real

Self abides within our Inner Shrine, patiently waiting for us to find Him and give recognition to His Presence there."

The Inner Shrine

The way to the Inner Shrine is found by means of interior spiritual experience, esoteric practices, sacramental grace, and initiation. Following the inner promptings of the Heart's homing signal, we are eventually led to this Inner Shrine or the Throne of the Deity. Here, in the Heart of Reality, we can build the Grail Cup within ourselves from the sacred triune substance of Chokmah (Wisdom), Binah (Compassion), and Tiphereth (Beauty and Harmony), from which we can imbibe the nectars and fragrances of Divine Gnosis.

The Divine Gnosis, the Gnosis Kardia is the straight knowledge of the Heart. It is that which cannot be taught, but which can only be learned. In *Mysteries of the Holy Grail*, Heline writes, "Thus the old legend shows that the New Age man figured in Parsifal will build the Grail Cup within himself, and that the Castle which houses it is the body, which is indeed the Temple of the Grail and House of the Holy Spirit."

The Purpose of the Temple of the Holy Grail

Legend suggests the Holy Grail is found not by having the right answers, but by asking the right question, e.g., "Who does the Grail serve?" A warning is given, a hope is shared. The warning: to those who take up the Great Quest hoping for self-aggrandizement, the fogs of illusion will sooner or later descend and envelop one. The hope: the Grail Knight, the Bodhisattva, who does his or her practice for the benefit of all sentient beings, can (after years of striving) overcome the inner dragons, safely cross over the mote of treacherous emotional waters, and find his or her way to the Holy Chalice of spiritual sustenance and understanding.

To each seeker who undertakes the Great Quest, the Grail represents something unique. Each individual who sets out on the Quest can discover the Grail Castle within the Temple of his or her own Heart—or in Kabbalistic terms, Tiphereth. The experience of others is there as a guide, but only as a guide. Each must find his or her own way by following the promptings of the spirit within.

Frater Achad in *The Chalice of Ecstasy* writes, "And each must learn to travel this Path, each must overcome his own obstacles, unmask his own illusions. Yet there is always the possibility that others may help us to do this and, as in the case of Parzival led by Gurnemanz who had traveled that Way before, we may be guided in the true Path and taught to avoid the many false byways that may tempt us in our search for the Temple of the Holy Grail."

Chivalric selfless service was the code of the Medieval Knight of the Grail. In this same spirit, the purpose and work of the Temple of the Holy Grail is to spiritually empower those committed to the ways of subtle interior and proactive exterior chivalric service.

The anonymous, invisible service commitment of those working in the T∴H∴G∴ is to daily send forth the subtle energy of Blessings to all beings. One begins to learn to "hold" and wield the Christ energy of the *San Graal* or Sangreal and direct it from within the consciousness of the High Self. This can be done sacramentally as well.

The Divine Christ

In simplest terms, the Divine Christ is a collective figure for the perfection of humanity. The Christ is humanity perfected, and dwells latent in every human Heart. Every human being is an emanation of Godhead and contains within his or her Heart the Divine Spark or Seed. Thus each person is a Christ in the making.

Mar Yeshua, the Master Jesus

While there are many Masters and many White-Robed Circles, the T∴H∴G∴ is a Priestly White-Robed Lodge of the Christ under the Master Jesus. For us as Templars, our guide, model, and Hierophant is our Elder Brother, the Master Jesus. For us He symbolizes our best and highest human Self. We know that the Divinity which manifested in Master Jesus differs in development, but not in quality, from that which is latent in each one of us. He is the Great Example, not the exception. As Ellwood states in *The Cross and the Grail,* "He represents the pilgrim self that is the ultimate source of all our highest aspects as they reflect the inner divine, our most authentic personality." We are, as He was, children of the Most High in whom we live and move and have our being, described by Hermes as an "intelligible sphere whose center is everywhere, and circumference nowhere."

Our view of Master Jesus is grounded in an alternative image that flows from contemporary biblical research, esoteric streams of Christian mysticism, and Western Mystery schools. For those who study in the Temple, the focus is not about "believing in" Jesus but rather to being in a relationship with his teachings and with the same Spirit he seemed to know so intimately. The experience of others is there as a guide, but only as a guide. Each must find their own way by following the promptings of the Spirit within. Ours is an Hermetic, Gnostic, and Kabbalistic view. We emphasize discovering the Holy Spirit of Wisdom and Compassion within—the school mistress of all disciples.

The Divine Will, Pattern, Plan, or Grail for Humanity

The Holy Grail is the eternal *Graal,* the sacred way or gradual upward path of initiation. It is built into all Reality—macrocosm and microcosm. The Freemasonic understanding of God as the Great Architect of the Universe, Who designs upon His trestleboard and then causes the Blueprint or Plan to be implemented knowingly or unknowingly by both positive and negative forces, reflects this teaching of the Grand Grail as the Divine Plan.

Alice Bailey, writing about the Divine plan in *Ponder on This,* says "The first thing to be grasped, is that there is a Plan for humanity, and that this Plan has always existed." In the booklet *Hierarchy,* Torkom Saraydarian shares his understanding of the Divine Plan by writing, "The Plan can be sensed in the age-long history of the continents, civilizations, and cultures. It can partly be read in the course of the evolutionary Path." He goes on to describe the immediate goals of the Divine Plan as suggested by the Tibetan Master D.K. These goals include:

1. To bring to an end the age-long spirit of separativeness in our religious and national attitudes.
2. To prepare the way for the reappearance of the Christ.
3. To clean the polluted air, water, and soil all over the earth.
4. To provide enough food, adequate housing, and clothes for everyone, everywhere.
5. To provide conditions for the total liberation of women all over the world.
6. To utilize sound and color scientifically to bring about the aligning of the Ego, the influencing of groups, the making of contact with Hierarchy, the cooperation with the devas in order to further the constructive ends of evolution.

7. To make humanity a center of energy, a distributor of light, love, and divine will.

8. To awaken a greater sense of responsibility in the heart of the human being.

9. To organize groups which will work for the one humanity, as sensitive agents between Hierarchy and humanity.

10. To reveal new methods of healing.

11. To spread the spirit of harmlessness into the hearts of all.

We agree with Bishop Saraydarian that the Great Invocation provides a sketch of the Divine Plan for the immediate cycle. Here is a gender-free paraphrase of the Great Invocation applied as a *Great Evocation* intoned by means of harmonic principles, as used in T∴H∴G∴:

"From the Point of Light within the mind of God,
Light streams forth into the minds of All.
Light descends upon Earth.

"From the point of Love within the Heart of God,
Love streams forth into the Hearts of All.
Christ returns to Earth.

"From the Center where the Will of God is known,
Purpose guides our little wills,
That Purpose which the Masters know and serve.

"From the center which we call the human race,
The Plan of Love and Light emanates outward.
It seals the door where evil dwells.

"Light, Love, and Purpose hallow the Grail on Earth."

The Temple in the 21st Century

In the next chapter we will describe the remarkable events that led to the re-awakening of true initiatic Templar orders of the Grail and the establishment of the Temple of the Holy Grail.

The Temple of the Holy Grail now stands fully operational as a vessel to serve the New Humanity, as a repository of initiatic wisdom both old and new, and as a powerful Mystery School for the 21st century. It is the renewal of the Holy *Graal* (literally, the Sacred "Gradual" or Graded Path of Initiation) reconstituted, upgraded, and revised for the New Humanity.

Recommended Books (available at www.WesternEsotericBooks.com)

Achad, F. (1923). The Chalice of ecstasy. Illinois: Yogi Publication Society.

Bailey, A. (1971). *Ponder on this.* New York: Lucis Publishing Company.

Boyer, G. & Keizer, L. (1994). *Collected writings of Richard Duc de Palatine.* CA: Privately Published.

Corinne, H. (1986). *Mysteries of the holy grail.* CA: New Age Bible and Philosophy Center.

Ellwood, R. (1997). *The cross and the grail: Esoteric Christianity for the 21stcentury.* Illinois: Quest Books.

Saraydarian, T. (1975). *Hierarchy and the Plan.* AZ: Aquarian Educational Group.

Saraydarian, T. (1991). *The Flame of the Heart.* CA: TSG Publishing Foundation.

CHAPTER TWO
RENEWAL OF THE
GRAIL BLESSING

The 19ᵗʰ Centennial Outpouring of the Grail

I n the late 1800's a secret English Templar order was in possession of an ancient Jewish terra cota cup, now encased in gold, and two silver auxiliary Grails. This gold cup was believed to be the true Eucharistic vessel of the Last Supper. The Templar order prepared to do the sacred Grail Rites that had been done once each century by the order and its predecessors in the year '88 (the mystical Christian Kabbalistic number). The purpose of the rite was to re-empower a channel for Divine Blessing upon the planet for the coming century and protect humanity from being overwhelmed by dark forces. It was the centennial outpouring of the Grail Blessing upon humanity.

The abbot of the order was an elderly man with great concern that the Grail chalices would be stolen by people who wished to use them for magical purposes. The chalices were secretly transported to London, where the centennial rite (a theurgical Eucharist) was performed. In spite of all precautions, the hiding place of the Grail Chalice was discovered.

Not many years after, all three chalices were stolen and used for black magical purposes. The chalices were again stolen from the thieves, the gold of the True Chalice melted down, and the pottery cup smashed into the earth. One other auxiliary chalice turned up at an antiquities auction in Antioch and was purchased by the Metropolitan Museum in New York. This chalice is now exhibited as the "Chalice of Antioch" with legends of it having been the true Holy Grail. The third silver chalice has never been found and may still be in the hands of self-seeking occultists.

The 20ᵗʰ Centennial Outpouring of the Grail

In the 1980's, after decades of unique spiritual training and progress, the Grailmaster, who knew nothing of the events described above, responded to interior guidance to construct a special chalice through white magical and theurgical preparations. This preparation, which included gathering of special materials from distant locations in seven sacred journeys required several years to complete. In August of 1988, when the prototype of the Eucharistic Chalice had been assembled, he was inspired to make an eighth journey without any knowledge of the final destination. This took him over a thousand miles to a certain sacred site in Canada in order to use the Chalice for a powerful theurgical Eucharist to bless the planet and humanity.

This was a time of extreme ordeal during which his life was threatened several times and he was under constant psychic, psychological, and physical attack. He has never revealed the details of what transpired, but against all odds he succeeded in carrying out the mission. Although he had no conscious understanding of the historical significance of what he was guided to do, he performed a theurgical Eucharistic rite in which the Sacrament was poured upon the earth as a planetary blessing. This was done on the eighth hour of the eighth day of the eighth month of the eighth year of the eighth decade of the century—August 8, 1988, at 8:00 A.M. Greenwich time. On the return trip, he heard an interior voice addressing him as *Graalmeister*, "Grailmaster"—a term unfamiliar to him, although he was well aware of the Grail legends.

The Grailmaster had suffered deep wounds both physical and emotional in this ordeal. He dragged himself home weak and debilitated. Immediately upon his return, however, his attention was drawn to a notice that a certain Tibetan Lama was visiting Santa Cruz and would be giving an empowerment through his interpreter. He felt strongly urged to attend.

This Lama was trained in subtle medicine and esoteric arts in the tradition of the Panchen Lama and had survived fifteen years in a Chinese prison before escaping to Italy, where he now resided. He had been guided to visit Santa Cruz at the time coinciding with the Grailmaster's return. When the two men met, there was immediate recognition between them. The Lama, who spoke no English, gave the Grailmaster precious pills without charge to bring back his physical and emotional health. Instead of just receiving the public empowerment, he found himself receiving intense telepathic instruction both from and through the Lama.

After this, the Lama returned to Italy, but he continued to assist and facilitate the Grailmaster's telepathic instruction, which came in lucid dreams, meditation, and various openings of knowledge. Much of this concerned esoteric methods for initiates to protect themselves against attacks of the same dark forces that had wounded him so badly—training which the Grailmaster would eventually adapt for others as the First Empowerment of the First Order in the Temple of the Holy Grail.

Shortly after this, the Grailmaster was astounded to discover a written account of the centennial Grail Blessing that had been done in 1888 by the English Templar order (now defunct) exactly one hundred years before his work. The narrative can be found in an article in *At the Table of the Grail*, edited by Matthews. Finally, the Grailmaster began to realize what he had been privileged to do, why his mystical ordeal had been necessary, and the meaning of his investiture with the title, Grailmaster.

He understood that dark forces had prevailed over the 20th century in ways that threatened the very survival of the planet and humanity. But Hierarchy had now provided a new vessel for the centennial Grail Blessing, which was accomplished on schedule for the 21st century. The Grail vessel, however, *was not the physical chalice that the Grailmaster had constructed.* It was a body of powerful initiatic transmission that was now poised to take form through the Grailmaster who now began the esoteric work of theurgically creating the *Eggregore* of a renewed initiatic *Graal* order. This new order was to be designated the Temple of the Holy Grail.

Building the Eggregore of the Temple

What is an eggregore? An *Eggregore* is a noetic or mental-spiritual group entity created by the minds, hearts, and life-work of many people—something like an astral body, but far more substantial. By way of example, the Roman Catholic Church has a powerful *eggregore*, for good or for evil, albeit somewhat unconscious. But every self-aware esoteric order establishes a weak *eggregore* even in its first generation that can be strengthened over the decades.

The Grailmaster realized that the Temple of the Holy Grail was not to be just another new-age group. Rather, it was to emerge as a powerful initiatic entity being synthesized by the impulses of Spiritual Planetary Hierarchy from existing, medieval, and forgotten mystery schools whose potencies were not dead, but merely dormant. These were not only Western and European, but Eastern, Middle Eastern, and shamanic schools. It was to be an enduring Mystery School for the New Humanity that would grow and develop through many generations of leadership.

Over the next few years, the Temple *Eggregore* was established and strengthened through shamanic magical and priestly theurgical operations as well as formal warrants and charters granted by existing authorities. These included the full repertoire of twenty-two lines of Apostolic Succession, the full repertoire of twenty-two esoteric European Templar, Rosicrucian, Illuminist, and Masonic orders of the Pan-Sophic Rites, as well as Chivalric and Martinist authorities for T:.H:.G:. In a few short years, the Temple of the Holy Grail became one of the most fully pedigreed esoteric orders in the Western world, and the *Eggregore* of the Temple quickly gained vigor and potency.

Apostolic Lineages of the Temple

The Grailmaster was already a lineage holder of most of the extant lines of valid Apostolic Succession from *Mar Yeshua*, the Master Jesus. This Priesthood is known as the Order of Melchizedek and is held by every legitimate Eastern Orthodox and Roman Catholic bishop.

The lineages are as follows: the better known Roman Catholic, Old Catholic, and Syrian-Antiochene, each flowing through the Apostle Peter; and the lesser known Coptic, Armenian, Greek Orthodox, Greek Melchite, Syro-Chaldaean, Chaldaean Uniate, Anglican, Irish, Welsh, French Non-Juring Bishops, Mariavite, Russian Orthodox, Syrian-Malabar, Syrian-Gallican, and Corporate Reunion, which includes three more. To these lineages, Bishop Boyer added the clandestine Gnostic Apostolic Hieratic lineage of the French Templars dating from the seventeenth century when he visited the Grailmaster in Santa Cruz and they performed a mutual subconditional consecration to share all Apostolic lineages with each other. All these twenty-two lines of extant Apostolic Succession now flow through the Home Temple Priesthood established as a distance learning seminary for ordination by the Grailmaster in 1998, and through all of the Bishops Templar of the T:.H:.G:.. Details of the lineages are published through **http://www.HomeTemple.org**.

Esoteric European Lineages of the Temple

Immediately following these events, the Grailmaster was contacted by Bishop George Boyer of London, an extremely sensitive world server and successor of Richard, Duc de Palatine, a great Gnostic Bishop. In dreams Boyer had been notified of the new initiatic impulse entrusted to the Grailmaster. He was guided to transmit to the new Temple all of the charters, titles, and authorities necessary to preserve the esoteric European lineages deriving from older *Graal* traditions. Two years later, Boyer would travel to Santa Cruz, California, to physically confirm transmission of the lineages and other authorities to the Grailmaster, which he now granted by written documents. Under the auspices of the Temple of the Holy Grail and the Grailmaster, Bishop Boyer began to undertake the new Initiations and Empowerments as they developed. He both studied and contributed to the Teachings that flowed through the Grailmaster.

Here is an outline of the charters and other authorities that Bishop Boyer conferred upon the Grailmaster. First are the twenty-two charters of the Pan-Sophic Rites of Freemasonry that were synthesized from all European esoteric orders extant at the end of the nineteenth century by John Yarker, Grand Master of the London Lodge and initiator of Mme. Blavatsky as a Master Mason.

The Ill. Bro. John Yarker, Jn.: 33, 90, 96, Initiated and Installed James Heard as the first Vicarius Salomonis, Conservator of the Rite of the Ancient Universal Pan-Sophic Rite of Masonry, who transmitted to Ill. Bro. Hugh G. deWillmott, who transmitted to H.S.H. Duc de Palatine, who transmitted to Bishop and Count George Boyer, Grand Archon, Brotherhood and Order of the Pleroma, Hermetic Brotherhood of Light, Sanctuary of the Gnosis (which have authority to transmit the following extant lineages), who warranted the Grailmaster, on behalf of the Temple of the Holy Grail, to carry forth the authorities embodied in the Pansophic Rite, including:

- **ILLUMINIST (ULTRA-MASONIC):**
  1. *Fratres Lucis* or Brotherhood of the Illuminati
  2. Order of the Illuminati
  3. Order of the Martiniste
  4. Brotherhood of Luxor
- **TEMPLAR:**
  1. Knights of the Holy Ghost
  2. Knights of St. John

3.   Knights of Malta
4.   Knights of the Holy Sepulchre
5.   Knights of the Temple

- **ROSICRUCIAN:**
  1.   Order of the True Rosy Cross
  2.   Golden and Rosy Cross
  3.   The Order of the True Rosy Cross
- **GNOSTIC ECCLESIAE:**
  1.   Order of the *Ecclesiae Rosicrucianae Catholicae* (Catholic)
  2.   Hidden Church of the Holy Grail (Protestant, Edgar Waite)
- **ULTRA-MASONIC and MASONIC:**
  1.   Ancient and Primitive Rite
  2.   Rite of Memphis
  3.   Rite of *Mizraim*
  4.   Ancient and Accepted Scottish Rite
  5.   Swedenborgian Rite
  6.   Order of the *Rose-Croix* of Hiredom
  7.   Order of the Holy Royal Arch of Enoch
- **CHIVALRIC:**

To these have been added a Chivalric Order. Admission to the +OMR+ (Teaching, Healing, and Chivalric Order of St. Michael and St. Raphael) is automatically conferred by document upon those who are accepted and self-initiated into T:.H:.G:. They are automatically advanced to the status of Companion when they complete the Healer Empowerment of the First Order. Those who successfully complete the Seven Self-Empowerments of the First Order are qualified to be dubbed Knights or Dames in a T:.H:.G:. gathering or seminar with Grail Mother and Grailmaster, who is Knight Commander of the Order. Their names will be formally added to the official lists of European nobility. Bishop Boyer is Abbott of the Order, which was chartered by Prince August, last descendent of the Emperor Hohenstaufen, Grand Master of the Pactio Secreta that constituted all chivalric orders of the twelfth century, both Christian and Islamic.

However, the titles Knight and Dame are *not* hereditary. In T∴H∴G∴ nobility is considered to be a *spiritual quality* that must be earned for recognition in each individual. Thus, it is the policy of the Order that these titles, while they are legal and recognized among all chivalric orders, are conferred only upon an individual and cannot be transmitted to offspring.

- **MARTINIST:**

In addition to the charters and warrants transmitted to the Grailmaster by Bishop Boyer, he also received valid authority as a Free Initiator, or S∴I∴IV, of the Martinist orders through a transmission from the French +OMCC+. This made him a full and independent Initiator, under the auspices of no organization. Certain Martinist and Ultra-Masonic schools welcome women equally with men. Therefore, the Grailmaster decided that the Temple would transmit the Martinist Initiations in its First Order.

The M∴O∴T∴ (Martinist Order of the Temple) offers all three of the Martinist Philosophical Degrees through S∴I∴III (*Superior Inconnu III* or "Anonymous Adept of the Third Degree"). The Martinist training is useful, and members of the T∴H∴G∴ First Order who wish to study in the *Elus Cohen* Kabbalistic theurgical school of +OMCC+ are referred and given recommendations to an operative group.

As Bishop Boyer said recently in a convocation at his home in London where Grailmaster and Grail Mother were guests, "The reason the Temple of the Holy Grail has to be taken seriously is that its Empowerments *really do work*. I have done a great many esoteric spiritual practices in my seventy-odd years, but I have never found anything to compare with the power and efficacy of the Temple Empowerments. It is in *that fact* that the true authority of the Temple lies."

After his contact with the Lama, the Grailmaster began to receive an outpouring of details concerning the Empowerments that he was to share in meditations, dreams, and inspirations. Some were self-empowerments that he had already achieved that would be now organized in such a way as to make them transmissible. Others he was yet to achieve.

Here is the history of how the Grailmaster established and developed the *Eggregore* of the Temple of the Holy Grail.

The Sacred Temple Talisman

By means of channeled writings through Bishop Marie Lumazar, the Grailmaster received the first part of a technique for creating what would be called the Temple Talisman. This sacred Talisman was created from the earth of certain sacred places brought up from seven inches below the surface, spring water of other sacred places, rosemary harvested on a full moon, consecrated Pomegranate juice, and other elements used with certain blessings and processes. Lumazar's writings revealed that this technique was adapted from forgotten ancient Atlantean geomancy.

The Grailmaster was guided to synthesize the Talisman using elements gathered from sacred locations on a grand counter-sunwise circumambulation that led him from California through the Grand Canyon, Colorado, Canada, and down through Washington and Oregon. In each location, he intoned an invitation to the wisest of resident elemental beings to join the work of the Grail, link to the Temple through the elements of the Talisman, and serve as part of the *Eggregore* of the Temple. Through other theurgical techniques too complex to summarize, he linked the Talisman to the Kerubim of the Temple—Boosgreal, Drakongreal, Leongreal, and Anthroposgreal.

The completed Talisman became a powerful physical means of accessing the *Eggregore* of the Temple, and a vessel through which empowerments and other transmissions (normally requiring hands-on and physical presence or *darshan*) could be transmitted at a distance by merely sending and receiving the Talisman.

The Grailmaster sent three Talismans to the Lama in Italy and requested that he keep one Talisman as a blessing and transmit through the other two Talismans authority for the Grailmaster to develop the Long Life

Empowerment for the Temple on its own Western terms. Two weeks later the two Talismans were returned with a letter from the Lama's interpreter saying that he had agreed to the transmission and had authorized the Grailmaster to develop the Long Life Empowerment as he wished.

Who is the Grailmaster?

Before a person is able to carry out the kind of advanced spiritual work that the Grailmaster undertook, he or she must have lived a life of such length and quality that the requisite interior mental, emotional, and character elements necessary for Hierarchy to use have been developed. Today you will find him listed in *Who's Who in the World, Who's Who in Religion, Who's Who Among America's Teachers, The International Dictionary of Biography, Community Leaders and Noteworthy Americans,* and other such distinguished records. He is a respected Renaissance man of many talents and accomplishments. He might be compared to a sage like Emmanuel Swedenborg, who had also distinguished himself in society and lived to the half-century mark when his divine revelations began to come.

The Grailmaster was already a highly developed spiritual being nearly fifty years old when the events previously described transpired. He had earned his M.Div. degree in the Episcopal Divinity School at Cambridge, Massachusetts, during the Civil Rights era and had been an active political opponent of the Vietnam war and the draft.

He was an Episcopal Church Foundation Fellow, accepted at Princeton University for the doctoral program, but chose to do his work at the Graduate Theological Union in Berkeley, California—a consortium of graduate faculties of U.C. Berkeley, Stanford, and all of the academic theological seminaries of the Bay Area. While working on his doctoral dissertation, which was a translation, edition, and analysis of the Hermetic Initiation Tractate 6 of Nag Hammadi Coptic Gnostic Codex VI, he joined the faculty of the University of California at Santa Cruz in

Humanities, Religious Studies, and Classics. His dissertation is now a standard reference that is documented in contemporary Hermetic studies worldwide. He completed his Ph.D. in 1973.

In 1969 he met the women who would become his spiritual teacher, Mother Jennie Maiereder, and studied with her intensively until her death at the age of 97 years in 1975. During that time she introduced him to Manly Hall and many other significant spiritual occultists, and she taught him meditation and other practices. In 1975 she advised him to resign from the ministry of the Episcopal Church, where he had stayed his ordination as Deacon to serve as an unsalaried "Worker Deacon," and to accept the offer of ordination and consecration by Bishop Spruit as an independent bishop—an *episcopus vagans.* She told him that he should never be "under anyone's thumb," and be free to respond to his own invisible Teachers. In 1975, after Mother's death, the Grailmaster was ordained to the Priesthood and, a week later, consecrated to the Episcopate as a free and independent Bishop by Herrman Adrian Spruit.

At this time, the Grailmaster decided to cut his ties with academe and devote his studies and writings to esoteric spirituality. He became associated with Bishop Torkom Saraydarian, Bishop Warren Watters, and developed communications with Stephan Hoeller, Rosa Miller, and other Gnostic bishops. He wrote *The Authentic Jesus*, his occult novel *The Astral Man* (now published in co-authorship with Bishop Eugene Whitworth, author of *The Nine Faces of Christ*), and other works.

He established a unique private school for mentally gifted students serving students PreK-12. It gained worldwide recognition and was the subject of news features by the *London Times, 60 Minutes, Good Morning America,* and many other media. He administered as Headmaster and taught full time in the classroom for twenty years, innovating curriculums and establishing a highly effective methodology for educating mentally gifted students. Scores of America's most brilliant young people passed through his mentorship.

The Grailmaster was also a talented musician, performing both symphonic and jazz trumpet. He founded the Santa Cruz Chamber Orchestra and the New Hastings Symphonic Band, which he conducted for seven seasons, producing an award winning sound track for the new version of *Peter and the Wolf* that is now used in many elementary schools. The film, starring Ray Bolger, won the CBS Children's Film Festival awards and a Cannes Film Festival award. He composed music and introduced new music of other American, Canadian, and South American composers, as well as producing the Nutcracker Ballet every year, the Messiah Sing-Along, and serving on boards for many musical and theatrical arts organizations and the musicians union. The Grailmaster's son Rafael became one of America's top young cellists.

The Grailmaster was also an accomplished jazz musician and had been asked to found the U.C.S.C. Jazz Program. He had credentials in all areas of jazz, performing in concert and at international jazz festivals with a gamut of musicians from Sonny Stitt, Chet Baker, and Scott Hamilton to dixieland all-stars like Jake Stock, Big Tiny Little, and the 10th Avenue Jazz Band.

During the 1980's, the Grailmaster established communications with many spiritual seekers and accepted students for private ordination training. He was one of the first to consecrate women bishops, and soon he found himself mentoring a large number of men and women who wished to advance in independent Holy Orders. He wrote extensively, circulating his writings privately among students. In 1985 he was guided to translate the historical Teachings of the Master Jesus in the form of a new Gospel called, *The Simple Word of the Master Jesus.* He dedicated the completed work in a gathering with close spiritual associates on January 1, 1986. That summer, he was given a Tibetan mantra with prostrations to the Christ as the Lama, which he carried out for two months, after which he was telepathically given the information on harmonic intoning and chanting—theory, practices, and techniques he privately published in *Esoteric Principles of Song and Chant.* This is now part of the Temple Teachings.

He had been doing a great deal of writing, but at this point he vowed to stop writing and do nothing but practice. He wanted to leave behind discursive modalities and work with pure *gnosis*. He stopped writing for four years and devoted his time to long retreats in the wilderness, meditations, and the leading of groups in such activities.

In 1985 Barbara Marx Hubbard, whom he later consecrated as a Bishop, asked him to bring together a group of people to co-create the first December 31st Global Peace Meditation. He initiated the project and at 4 A.M. Pacific Standard Time (Greenwich Mean Noon) on December 31, 1986, the Santa Cruz Civic Auditorium was filled with two thousand people and many others outside unable to get in for an uninterrupted one-hour meditation coordinated with other groups from Moscow to Africa. There were other huge gatherings at the Kingdome in Washington state, the Civic Auditorium in Denver, and worldwide. The Grailmaster's group continued the annual meditation for many years after, until it finally evolved as a private ritual done by a small number of highly aware individuals able to operate on the *Eggregore* of December 31st created worldwide by hundreds of thousands of participants. He also led Harmonic Convergence, Wesak, and many other rituals and gatherings during this period.

Today the Grailmaster works in educational administration. Among other things, he serves as Academic Dean for Great Western University in San Francisco, working with Drs. Eugene and Ruth Whitworth to develop academic courses and degree programs based upon the study and practice of Western and Eastern mystery and initiatic traditions. The web site for Great Western University is located at **http://www.GreatWesternUniversity.org**

The Stigmata of Master Hilarion

One of the most significant events in the Grailmaster's development was symbolized by stigmata that appeared on his hands after an all-night vigil in the Library of the Halcyon Theosophical Community near San Juan, California. This was established by Blavatsky's New York group in 1889, and the Library still possesses the chair that Blavatsky sat upon to teach.

After the vigil, when the sun was beginning to rise, the Grailmaster observed very pronounced red welts appearing on the top of both hands between thumb and forefinger. Within a few minutes they had developed into a symbol measuring about 1.25 inches square. It was finely formed, almost like a tattoo, but raised like a welt, and fiery red. It looked like an "H" with a tail, like the astrological sign for Uranus, but with a curve and an arrow on the end. The image on each hand was a mirror reflection of the other.

When he returned home, one of his students photographed the stigmata, which remained visible for over a week. During this time he found the exact symbol in a book by Ann Ree Colton, the Los Angeles psychic and spiritual teacher. She described this as the symbol of the Master Hilarion. This was astounding because the Ascended Master associated with the Halcyon community is Hilarion. He is said to be the Master that oversaw the founding and still oversees the development of the community.

Hilarion (Ilarion) was a Greek adept that Blavatsky deeply respected. She alludes to meetings with him in several of her writings, and notes that after a certain time he left the Western world and disappeared. The implication is that he returned to Tibet where he completed practices that perfected him as a Master.

The Grailmaster feels that he was brought under the special guidance of Hilarion at this time, and that the unfoldment of all the work that led to the founding of the Temple of the Holy Grail in the late 1980's and early 1990's was primarily under Hilarion's oversight. He also feels that the Lama who assisted him after the Grail ordeal was guided by Hilarion.

In the next chapter, we present an overview of Christian Gnosis and a summary of essential Gnostic teachings.

CHAPTER THREE
CHRISTIAN GNOSIS AND THE
GRAIL

Secret Initiatic Tradition

The original Teachings of *Mar Jeshua*, the Jewish Master Jesus, were Gnostic and Kabbalistic, that is, initiatic and oral. These were the "Chrestian" Teachings, as they were known in some of the earliest references to the new religion. They were carried on within the inner circle of those personally initiated by Jesus who practiced the modality of transmission used in the Mysteries of Hermes Trismegistus—that is, the Egyptian mysteries. This is clear from the fragments of the letter from Clement of Alexandria quoting from the so-called *Secret Gospel* written by Mark, the closest disciple of Peter, and other documents produced in the context of the Christian Mysteries such as the *Gospel of Thomas* and the *Gospel of Mary* (Magdelene).

In the dominical sayings transmitted through the four canonical gospels (which are exoteric or non-initiatic documents) we find clues about the oral or Kabbalistic inner tradition, sometimes known as the Apostolic Gnosis, transmitted by the Master Jesus. For example, in the book of Mark, verse 10 we read, "When He was alone, they that were about Him, with the Twelve, asked of Him the parables. And He said unto them, 'To you is given the mystery of the Kingdom of God; but unto them that are without, all things are done in parables.'" He warned them not to "cast your pearls before swine, lest they turn and rend you."

The Inner Circle

Mar Yeshua, the Master Jesus, had *talmidim* or disciples far and wide. His disciples included women (as it is clear from the Acts of the Apostles). He separated his disciples into seventy apostles whom he sent forth, into a close group of about seventeen (the traditional "twelve"), and into smaller groups. One of these smaller groups included Peter, James, and John. They witnessed the so-called transfiguration event, which was actually a phenomenon of advanced *Merkabah* mystic ascent and communion with the Jewish Masters Moses and Elijah.

Other close disciples included his brother James, beloved Lazarus, John, Mary Magdelene, Salome, and Thomas, each of whom he initiated and instructed separately according to individual abilities and understanding. James he initiated into the mysteries of High Priesthood and sacred intoning of divine names. Mary Magdelene, who was not a harlot (as the later patriarchal churches tried to portray her) but a Jewish Sibyl or Prophetess, he "begot" by raising her in rebirth through the seven *Shamayim* or Heavens.

Jesus also had colleagues such as John the Baptist who showed certain affinities with Essene and Dead Sea communities, as did the earliest communities of Jesus' disciples after the Resurrection event.

Initiatic Sects

At the time of Master Jesus there were several initiatic sects in Palestine and Egypt, such as the Gymnosophists ("Naked Philosophers") or community of Hindu yogis living in Egypt, the Therapeutai ("Healers"), the Dositheans (followers of Dositheus), at least two kinds of Essene community, and the Mandaeans ("Knowers, Gnostics"), whose sect originated with John the Baptist, among others.

The chief extant writings of the Mandeans, who were driven out of their homeland by persecution, date from seventh and eighth centuries and include the *Ginza* or Treasure. Their teachings are not unlike those of Manes and the Manichaeans that were so important to St. Augustine of Hippo before his conversion to Catholic Christianity, but they probably reflect the Gnosis of the Johannite Church, with which they seem to have a historical relationship. The Mandaeans of Iraq have been hostile toward Christianity since Byzantine times, when it was no longer safe for its communities to dwell in the Holy Roman Empire.

According to them, the human soul is imprisoned in the grand illusion of matter, but can be freed by *Manda da Hayye*, the Gnosis of Life, sometimes personified as the Redeemer *Hibel* or *Enos Uthra*, who led an incarnate life on earth and defeated the powers of darkness, and who is now the Gnostic Psychopomp or guide of souls, like Hermes and Thoth.

The prophet Mani founded what would be known as Manichaeism in Iran. It was perhaps the most popular and widely practiced form of Gnostic Christianity. The prophet Mani was flayed (skin stripped from his body) and torn into pieces, but his form of Christianity persisted because it did not come under the power of the Byzantine Church. Eventually it became a strong influence in Eastern Europe upon the Bogomiles and Cathari or "Pure Ones," whose communities in Southern France flourished under Merovingian rule.

Early Christianity

Christianity was a mélange of persecuted cults whose membership ranged from highly educated Roman and other citizens to illiterate slave devotees. Their beliefs and practices ranged from ascetic to licentious for the first three centuries, during which time the original Jewish context for the teachings of Jesus was expunged, forgotten, and replaced with Greek and other gentile myths, legends, and archetypes. Master Jesus was cast into the mold of a Middle Eastern savior deity, and the focus became Christology and theology rooted in Greek philosophy. When Constantine became its champion and established the Byzantine Empire in Asia Minor, however, it became official state religion practically overnight.

To make it worthy of such honor, Constantine demanded that it produce one official Bible, one Creed, and one acceptable doctrine. Why? Because there was, in the fourth century, no single unified Church. There were many regional, cultural churches in Rome, Egypt, Asia Minor, Palestine, Greece, each with different sets of Scripture, different rites, different theologies, and even different dates for Easter. For this reason, the Church Councils of Bishops from all major cities were convened.

The Ecumenical Council of Bishops

These Councils were not gatherings of sages, but of ecclesiastical leaders with many separate agendas. Their final decisions on doctrine, Scripture, and practice over many decades of different councils were at best political compromises, and at worst regional domination and cultural chauvinism.

Doctrines like reincarnation, which were taught in many churches from earliest times, were banned. Saints like Arius, whose apostles had introduced Christianity to Europe, and Origen, whose presentation of the Christian mysteries is still perhaps the greatest treasure of the Church Fathers, were condemned. The Roman dating for Easter was adopted.

Some of the greatest of the early Christian writings were dropped because of their length or banned because of their teachings. These banned writings included (among others) the *Shepherd of Hermas, The Didache of the Twelve Apostles,* and the authentic epistles of Ignatius of Antioch and Clement of Rome. The longer and less authentic Western Text of the Lucan and other New Testament Scriptures were used to create the Byzantine version of the New Testament, which later became the basis for Jerome's translation of the Greek New Testament into vernacular

Latin as part of the new Vulgate Latin Bible that would serve Roman Catholicism for over a millenium.

The new state religion soon became corrupt. Byzantine Christianity served the needs of political and ecclesiastical institutionalism, but created a huge gap between lay people and their God. Even today, Orthodox religion separates the laity from the Sanctuary by *reredos* screens and performs much of the Eucharistic Liturgy hidden from view as a priestly act in isolation from the laity.

Johannite and Monastic Traditions

In Asia Minor, the Apostle John had established his school, known as the Johannite Church. It held the same Gnostic and Kabbalistic views that had been taught by the Master Jesus. The Johannites refused to accept the domination of the state church, which had abolished too many of its ancient Apostolic traditions.

The state church was unable to persecute or legislate against the Johannite Church because it was held in high regard by all Christians. Its clergy and priesthood were considered to be saints. So the Byzantine Church allowed the Gnostic Johannite Church to continue openly, in spite of the sometimes embarrassing criticism its clergy leveled against the corruption of the state church. However, only membership in the state church qualified people for government service. The Johannite Church remained a small, fringe establishment tolerated by government.

The establishment of the state church of the Holy Roman Empire, which had little contact with the actual city of Rome, occurred suddenly within one generation. Christians who had braved persecution now found themselves operating under a developing ecclesiastical hierarchy that provided little spiritual inspiration. The reaction to this condition produced a yearning for true sanctity and holiness among many. They sought out legendary Christian saints who lived in the Egyptian desert as *eremites* ("hermits") or solitary desert dwellers.

Desert Mothers and Fathers

The Desert Fathers, as they have been called (who also included Desert Mothers), lived in solitary caves. They spent their days and nights in prayer, contemplation, and physical asceticism. Psychism, miraculous healing, exorcism, and transmission of instantaneous enlightenment were attributed to them. Some had been prominent members of society, while others had been thieves and murderers before their conversion.

The life of a Christian hermit in the desert—deprived of food, focused in devotions, meditating all night in cemeteries—produced visions and various kinds of spiritual experience to which the new generation of Christians in the Holy Roman Empire aspired. Individually and in groups, people made their pilgrimage to the Egyptian desert hoping for an interview with a saint, or to be healed of a malady, or to receive a blessing to release from perceived curse.

Some of these pilgrims never returned home. They were accepted as disciples of an *abba* or *apa* (spiritual father), cleared their own caves or huts, and began the ascetic life. Unlike the Hindu or Buddhist saints and yogins, however, they lived not by begging or accepting food from lay devotees, but by plaiting and weaving mats of bullrushes and trading them for basic necessities at the nearest village.

Over time, certain great saints accepted many disciples, who banded together to form a community and erect common building and huts. Finally these communities became monasteries, or communities of "solitaries." They were under the guidance of an *abba* or Abbot. Eventually, the first Rule for such a monastery was developed by St. Pachomius, and the Western world saw the rise of Christian monasticism.

It was probably in a Pachomian monastery that what we now know as the Nag Hammadi Coptic Gnostic Library, with its Jung Codex, *Gospel of Thomas,* and initiatic document of the Egyptian priestly school of Hermes Trismegistus, was preserved, copied, and hurriedly stashed away to be hidden from bandits who may have slaughtered the monks. Clearly, the early monastic traditions of the Egyptian desert were heterodox and Gnostic in their spiritual orientation.

Not far from Nag Hammadi, in the city of Achmim, was established a new school of mystic Pythagorean and Empedoclean philosophy to preserve the arts of alchemy and theurgy. Among the members of this school were Christians of the esoteric Alexandrian school, who were no longer welcome in major cities controlled by the Holy Roman Empire. It was in Achmim that many of what would later be called the *Graal* traditions were preserved and transmitted to Islamic scholars. They, in turn, transmitted them to Europeans many centuries later.

The Single Nature of Christ

The inner Apostolic traditions of Jesus had been transmitted and perpetuated in Alexandria through Basilides, his son and dynastic successor Isidore, and on to Clement and Origen, with versions of the Teachings in Rome (Valentinus; the Valentinian Gnosis later appears allied to European traditions of the Rose Cross, as we will later mention). But the Gnostic churches of Egypt and the Middle East were driven underground by ecclesiastical authorities after Christianity became the state religion of the Byzantine Empire.

The great saint and *episcopus vagans*, Nestorius, awakened spirituality among the Egyptian Copts, just as Arius had done with the Europeans. But he and his doctrine of the single nature of Christ, as opposed to the Roman dual nature, was condemned by the Church Councils as Monophysitism. His Monophysites were Gnostic and Kabbalistic in that they regarded Christ as the true and original part of human nature—the Divine Spark of true human reality.

Great Gnostic psalms like the *Hymn of the Pearl* celebrate the unity of God and humanity in the same nature, viewing the souls of humanity and all manifestation as emanations in a stream from Godhead. They were philosophical monists, not dualists.

Christ was not of some different nature than humanity, but was the perfection of true and original human nature. Christhood was what Buddhism called the "Buddha nature" resident in all sentient beings. All people, and all beings, were Christs in the making according to the ancient Graal.

Christian Philosophical Dualism

It was at this time that philosophical dualism was bringing such departures from the teachings of Jesus as the Doctrine of Eternal Damnation into Christian theology. The very late apocryphal *Gospel of Nicodemus* portrays a Lake of Burning Pus into which all the enemies of Christ will be cast forever. This dualism helped to justify the persecution of older Hellenistic religions by zealots of the Church. After an interlude when so-called "pagan" religions (the traditional initiatic mysteries) were allowed under the enlightened Emperor Julian, Byzantine rulers sanctioned vigorous persecution of all non-Christian religions, including forms of Christianity that did not conform to the edicts of the Church Councils. The state religion of the Byzantine Empire set out to eradicate Gnostic, Manichean, Nestorian, Arian, and all other heresies.

The Egyptian Christians who clung to the basic tenet that humanity and divinity were of one nature were ostracized as "monophysites," adherents to the idea that Man, God, and Christ were united in one nature by the person of Jesus. Many of them emigrated to India, where their Nestorian or Monophysite Church still survives. The persecuted

Nestorians became great travelers and traders, bringing their heretical, Gnostical religion to many places of the East and Near East.

The memory of this persecution and the issue of the One Nature has never been forgotten. Even to this day, Gnostic priests give the Blessing and direct other forces through the right hand with the *single forefinger raised* to indicate the single nature of man and God, while the Catholics raise forefinger and middle finger to indicate the dual nature of Christ.

But the *Imitatio Christi* could not be stopped by persecution, so powerful was the spiritual impulse that lay behind it, and there was an exodus of hundreds to the deserts of Egypt. The Desert Fathers and Mothers cared not for priest or pope, spending their days in mystic exercises of purification and humility. Their forms of the Teaching are summarized for us in Thomas Merton's *Sayings of the Desert Fathers* excerpted from the voluminous *Philokalia* and other sources. They created the foundations for Christian monasticism, through which Europe was evangelized, written knowledge was preserved, and (by way of various monastic reforms) Gnosis was transmitted through great lights like St. Bernard of Clairvaux—patron to the Knights Templar, through whom the foundations of European Gnosis (Rosicrucian, Masonic, etc.) were laid.

The Home Temple Priesthood transmits the historical European Gnostic Apostolic lineage of the Gnostic Ecclesiae probably derived from the Johannite Church through the Knights Templar.

Brief Overview of the Gnostic-Hermetic Tradition

There have been two forms of the Gnostic-Hermetic tradition. The first approach is designated as pessimistic, i.e., the form that is totally negative about incarnate life and strives to release itself from it to return to its spiritual Home. In this older approach to high Gnostic practice (in Buddhist terms, the Way of the Arhat), the goal was to transcend cosmos through complete negation of ego, giving the impression of escape from the world.

It was associated with ascetic practices and avoidance of human affairs. It was perpetuated in the asceticism of Manichaeism and the religion of the medieval Albigensians.

The second approach is also negative about incarnate life but strives to sanctify it by bringing that spiritual Home into flesh (in Buddhist terms this is the Way of Mahayana and the Boddhisatva). In this later approach (the Way of the Boddhisatva), the goal was to overcome the human condition in order to remain and abide with humanity and all sentient beings, and to transform cosmos through the exercise of Divine Selfhood, Love, and Will as a colleague of Divine Hierarchy in the guidance of human affairs and the evolution of cosmos. Hermetic sciences, theurgy, astrology, geomancy, psychism, magic, and alchemical arts were practiced to spiritualize humanity and society, communicate with angels, and bring perfection into incarnate manifestation.

Use of Buddhist terminology is appropriate because Mahayana and the Bodhisattva ideal is not only parallel to the ideal of Gnostic Christhood and sainthood, but it developed at the same time in history. Many Gnostic scholars conclude that since the Egyptian desert mystics dwelt in communities near the Gymnosophists of India, there must have been extensive syncretistic exchange of ideas between East and West in the early Christian centuries, especially between Gnostics and Buddhists. In fact, the Gnostic teachings of the Apostle Thomas were established in the East primarily because Christian, Buddhist, and Hindu Gnosis are so closely related—probably through Pythagoras, who brought the Vedic wisdom of the Brahmins to Asia Minor and greatly influenced Socrates, Plato, and all subsequent Hellenic philosophers. Plato was a Pythagorean Initiate.

It is this knowledge of the unity of all humanity and all beings, this recognition that the seeming absence of God is merely a temporary blindness of perception, this understanding that there can be no meaning in separative existence and consciousness, that motivates the heart of every saint devoted to the Imitation of Christ to freely and spontaneously utter the Bodhisattva Vow—"We shall never abandon Thee. We are Thou, and Thou art We."

It is a higher octave of this latter Gnostic approach that we now emphasize in the Temple Teachings. Its recent antecedents are to be found in the many European Gnostic brother-and sisterhoods whose interest in the divine transformation of secular, human, and natural reality led them into experiments with alchemy, Hermetic talismanic magic, Kabbalistic operations, psychic group experiments such as those of the Elus Cohens and other Illuminists, and group liturgical operations such as the Ultra-Masonic and Egyptian rites.

A Summary of Essential Gnostic Teachings

• The Gnosis cannot be taught; it must be learned.

• The Gnosis or "Knowledge" is inscribed in the innermost heart of all humanity. It has thus existed from the most ancient of times and been realized and taught by Gnostics of all generations. It has been termed the *gnosis kardia*, the *scientia cordis*, the knowledge of the heart. It has been called "straight knowledge" and intuition. It requires no catechism or indoctrination, as human beings tend, in their most natural state, to eventually work out and attain Divine Gnosis through trial and error. The so-called Fall of Man is part of the Divine Plan and is not a sin, and the Serpent of the Genesis Adam and Eve legend is another Face of God.

• The vehicle of Divine Gnosis has been described as *Rigpa*, the I AM of Ain Soph Aur, the L.V.X., the Holy First Iliaster, the Nous of the Authentia, the Mind of Hermes, or of Christ. This vehicle (the Iliaster) is separated from our mundane consciousness by a veil of illusion. This illusory veil is known as cosmos—the created, reflected, or material world. We are not referring to the so-called natural world or of human or other physical-etheric bodies—mineral, vegetable, and animal. Rather, we refer to the limited, contracted, ego-centered perception of Divine Reality available to humanity in its condition of incarnation into matter. That condition is often called duality—the perception of "I and Thou," us and them, me and not-me, the inner and the outer which are, in reality, a "single One," as Jesus says in the *Gospel of Thomas*.

- Humanity is one primal Being, now separated and fragmented into the separatism of ego-consciousness by the illusions of duality. Primal Humanity has been called the Christ, the Son of the Unknown Father-Mother God. It has also been called Kosmos, for Primal Humanity as one Being is Kosmos, and each separate incarnate human being is a microcosm containing within its auric egg the complete Egg of the Universe in holographic, alchemical, magical resonance.

- Neither Humanity nor Kosmos are created—that is, formed out of some hypothetical substance separate from the Unknown Father-Mother God. Rather, the All is emanated in a Pleroma (Fullness) of Aeons (Archetypes) from the Father-Mother. Thus, Humanity is Divine, and Kosmos (as opposed to the human perception of Kosmos) is Humanity's divine macro-form. It is this primal unity between macrocosm and microcosm that is the basis for all so-called psychism, magic, and miracle. This was a Platonic doctrine deriving from Pythogorean teachings, and ultimately from Brahmin Vedic philosophy.

- The individual, incarnate human ego is like a royal prince or princess who has forgotten its origin and "knoweth not whence it came and whither it goeth." Yet he or she is the royal heir to the

Kingdom. When finally one has plumbed the depths of duality and filled oneself with the husks of illusion in the Kathodos or Downward Path into matter, one begins to glimpse a memory of who and what one truly is. The veil between God and humanity is partially rent, and one begins to yearn for the true Home. The individual then undertakes the Divine Quest that leads—precept upon precept, degree by degree—along the homeward journey, which is initiatic. (Cf. Jesus Parable of the Prodigal Son.) As one returns in the Anodos or Upward Initiatic Path, one brings with itself a host of other elemental and psychic beings intimately connected with its monadic individuality that has been projected through many incarnations and experience over aeons of time, for "man is the redeemer of matter," and "the whole creation groaneth and travaileth in pain" in expectation of the "manifestation of the Scions of God (St. Paul, Romans 8:19-23)."

• The means of human self-realization is anamnestic divine memory (Plato), for as each individual monad descends into matter it leaves a tracing or record in each of the invisible bodies and planes it must descend through before incarnation. These subtle spirillae are known collectively in Hindu yoga philosophy as the antahkarana, or psychic extensions of normal human sensory perception. By awakening and rebuilding these spirillae of higher psychic perception (not to be confused with the lower psychism of mediums and fortune-tellers), the Gnostic begins to develop continuity of consciousness on the higher, invisible planes of existence. He or she is then able to be conscious and serve as part of Divine Rule or Hierarchy in subtle bodies, to be awake while his or her body sleeps, to achieve communion with elementary, elemental, and angelic spirits, and to carry on the work of Divine Transformation while in flesh. This is the state of Jewish, Christian, and Hermetic saints, who dwell in the Ogdoad as

"Standing" Ones—the original meaning of the Aramaic term used by Jesus for Resurrection after physical death.

In the next chapter we present an overview of Medieval European Grail Legends. This will summarize historical background information required to appreciate events that led to the re-awakening of dormant initiatic orders when the Temple of the Holy Grail was established in 1988.

CHAPTER FOUR
MEDIEVAL EUROPEAN GRAIL
LEGENDS

It was during the eighth and ninth centuries that the *Graal* legends of Grailmaster Treverezent, the Cave and Mountain of Initiation, and the initiatic Grail school emerged. We hear of them in the context of the conflict between Merovingian and Carolingian forces. The Grail Mysteries seem to have been the inner school of Gnostic and Manichean Christianity. They were cross-cultural, knowing Islamic alchemical, Comacine mathematical, Hellenistic Hermetic, and Celtic magical traditions.

Later Arthurian romances glorify the Celtic aspects of mystic Christianity and symbolize the Grail as a Chalice containing not the Holy Blood, but the alchemical cosmic fluid of Divine Purity, Blessing, and Healing. The Germanic alchemical romances concerning Parsifal may better preserve something of the Merovingian roots in its emphasis upon the one pure and perfect knight—the symbolic child of Jesus. But we cannot learn much about the historical *Graal* mysteries from these later legends. They represent an emergence into the popular consciousness of hidden influences from an earlier time that were now coming to flower in the Renaissance.

However, based upon earlier legends about Charlemagne and his court, we can speculate that, despite its originally Merovingian setting, the *Graal* school eventually became the guiding spiritual light of the Carolingian Renaissance. Charlemagne and his descendants had no spiritual allegiance to the Papacy—merely a political negotiation. The uneasy dichotomy of Church and State that characterized the rise of the European nations already existed in the historical conflict between European tradition and Roman orthodoxy when Charelmagne was forced to stand for three days in the snow to humble himself before the Pope so that he could receive the Church's official coronation.

In the tenth and eleventh centuries the legendary Grail mysteries described in the Initiate Troubador Wolfram von Eschenbach's *Parsival* were developed by Carolingian adepts as they wrested the Celtic-Teutonic spiritual flame from the long-haired Merovingian dynasties and established the Chivalric orders and rules.

Warrior-Saints and spiritual masters like Hugo of Tours assumed the seat of the legendary Grailmaster Treverezent. The *Graal* or Grail Path was established within the institution of Chivalry, where it would later constitute the lynchpin of the inner mysteries for the Knights Templar.

The Pactio Secreta and the Chivalric Grail

In the twelfth century there was needed a grand corrective to the growing secular power of the Roman Pope, who was determined to gain both political and theological control of the Germanic territories as had already been established in Gaul. Frederick II von Hohenstaufen became that corrective force. He devoted his life to fighting Papal political rule out of the Germanic states, and is the main reason that Protestantism would later find protection and nurture among the German speaking people.

Von Hohenstaufen was perhaps the most brilliant and educated monarch who ever lived. Among his court and associates were the greatest alchemists and occultists of his day. He designed and operated the first submarine, which he used for exploring the ocean floor. He was determined that the world was not to be ruled by Roman Papal fiat, but by a kind of "United Nations" made up of Grand Masters of all chivalric orders, Christian and Islamic. In other words, he believed that true Initiates should consult to resolve problems and determine the future political course of the world—not the Roman religious hierarchy.

Although we cannot know details of Chivalric initiation, we can surmise that training in Knighthood of the twelfth century had become the repository of both European and Islamic Grail tradition. Knighthood was the higher spiritual and physical training for all qualified princes of royal houses. It was a secular spiritual institution that was chartered not by bishops or popes, but by a royal house. The later connection of Christian chivalric orders to the Church was soon to be innovated by the Knights Templar, but it did not exist at the time of von Hohenstaufen. Knighthood was not a religious order with allegiance to the Church, but an initiatic school of training with three major degrees of advancement, just as in Freemasonry.

Von Hohenstaufen assembled the grand masters of all chivalric initiatic orders, Christian and Islamic, in c. A.D. 1140 in his Castel del Monte in Apuleia, Italy. Treasure to build the "Castle on the Mountain" was found in a vision by a Saracen Knight upon the place where it was to be constructed.

The Castel del Monte was built upon a unique octagonal plan. It was to be used for a meeting of all chivalric Grand Masters once every three years to defend the world from Papal imperialism and to establish initiatic control of international affairs. The assembly of Initiates (which was known as the Round Table, after the Arthurian Grail legends) concluded what was to be known as the *Pactio Secreta*—the Secret Pact.

For a few years von Hohenstaufen's military forces repelled the Papal armies, but later von Hohenstaufen met military defeats. He was not only excommunicated, but in a magical ritual he and all his descendents were given an eternal Papal curse "to the last bastard." All records of the von Hohenstaufen royal line were systematically destroyed by the Vatican for seven hundred years and remained only in the private archives of other royal houses.

Although his resistance to papal intrusion in Germany created the traditions that allowed for the later rise and protection of Protestantism in Germany, he was unable to carry out the full vision of the Secret Pact.

T∴H∴G∴. First Order training admits candidates to the three degrees of the only known authentic chivalric order derived from the royal house of Von Hohenstaufen and the Pactio Secreta.

The Knights Templar

Later in the twelfth century a small group of Christian knights undertook vows of chastity and service to protect pilgrims to and from the holy city of Jerusalem, newly liberated from Moslem control in the early Crusades. They made their own pilgrimage to Jerusalem and joined forces with the Merovingian successor who, to appease public sentiment, had been granted a symbolic jurisdiction on Mount Zion, or the location where Solomon's Temple had once stood in Jerusalem. With him they estab lished the Priory of Sion (for Zion, but possibly also for Scion, in reference to the legendary son of Jesus). Hughe de Payen wrote the Rule of the new religious order, which was to be established as both a military and monastic community. It became the model for all future chivalric or "horse mounted" orders of Europe.

Although it was pledged in service to the Papacy, its allegiance was to Gnostic spirituality. The Templars made allies and exchanged knowledge with many non-Christian initiatic schools, integrating their wisdom into Templarism, and developed their own inner school in conjunction with training for the three initiatic degrees: Page, Companion, and Knight. Eventually the Knights Templar undertook the sacred work of building chapels and cathedrals all over Europe, using the French *Compagnions* or Masons as their architectual consultants and builders.

Their cathedrals were built at first in the Gothic style, but over a century or more innovations were developed that led to a renaissance in architecture. The holy sites for chapels, churches, and cathedrals were chosen by psychic and esoteric means every bit as sophisticated as Chinese *Fung Shue* and traditional as Celtic ley-line geometry.

Today the esoteric knowledge behind such monuments as *Chartres* Cathedral are evident to anyone entering awe-struck at the visual, mathematical, and accoustical perfection of these medieval holy places. They were designed to create mystical experience and generate divine epiphany and theophany in even the most unlettered soul.

The Johannites of Asia Minor or Christians of St. John had survived well into the medieval period. They are of particular interest to us because of their relationship with the Knights Templar according to the *Charter of Larmenius*.

The Charter of Larmenius

This was a document made public by Fabre-Palaprat in post-revolutionary France to reveal the clandestine Gnostic Apostolic Succession transmitted to the Knights Templar, to reveal their transmission of valid Apostolic Orders to the Priory of Sion and Templar Episcopate through Hughe de Payens, and to establish that Templar Jacques De Molay had in fact legitimately transferred his office of Grand Master to Larmenius, and not allowed it to come to an end with his martyrdom in the Inquisition. The Charter shows a complete lineage of clandestine Templar Grand Masters through the nineteenth century.

The first part of the document is in Greek and states that the Johannite Gnostics of Asia Minor under the Patriarch Theokletos transmitted their tradition and conferred their Apostolic lineage directly from St. John the Divine upon de Payens and the Templars in the year A.D. 1154. It furthermore states that the lineage given to St. John from the Master Jesus devolved originally from Mosaic times through the Essenes to Jesus, and that Jesus was not the originator, but the transmitter of what was even then an ancient sacred lineage—perhaps the Melchizedekian priesthood.

The *Charter of Larmenius* was carefully examined by the scholars M. Matter and Eliphas Levi, both of whom concluded that it was authentic, and that the Johannite Gnostics had historical connections to the Mandaean communities of modern-day Iraq.

The Charter was a basis for revival of the Knights Templar (OSMTH) in the Napoleonic era, but it was challenged and attacked by rival Masonic interests, who wanted to put forward Masonic Templarism as the most valid form, as well as by other antagonistic political interests. Today in Coil's *Masonic Encyclopedia* the *Charter of Larmenius* is described as a forged document. But modern scholars who have re-examined the document marvel at the forgery, if it so be, because it contains numerous internal and textual evidences of authenticity. It is as though an authentic document, perhaps held for centuries in Vatican records of the Inquisition, has been conflated with forged additions.

There are legends that a Greek Pythagorean order known later as the Pednosophs ("Teachers of Wisdom") trained and initiated Templar Knights in the "Chrestian" or pre-Christian mysteries associated with Apollonius of Tyana, Plato, and Pythagorus. It had been founded as a Pythagorean order outside Christianity in sixth-century Asia Minor.

The Pednosophs seem to have preserved the alchemical traditions of Zosimus, Cleopatra of Alexandria, and the neo-platonic schools of Plotinus, Porphyry, and Dionysius the Areopagite. They may have been affiliated with early Armenian mystery schools such as that remembered by Bishop Saraydarian, or with Eastern European Rosicrucian schools like that of the Bulgarian Beinsa (Peter) Duoma (Duenov) and his disciple, Aivanhov.

The Knights Templar broke from the Priory of Sion in an amicable covenant. The Priory, which was essentially Merovingian but with allegiance to the Papacy, continued separately as the esoteric wing of the Vatican. According to records compiled by Bishop Bertil Persson, current Chaplain to OSMTH (the Templar order through Larmenius), some of the Grand Masters of the secret Priory have been such remarkable men as Botticelli, Leonardo Da Vinci, Robert Fludd, Sir Isaac Newton, Victor Hugo, and Claude Debussy. In truth, we know that the Priory withered into an insignificant monastic order that did not survive into modern times.

The Decimation of the Templar Order

The Templar Order was suddenly decimated two hundred years later when Phillip the Fair of France conspired with the Pope to take all their leadership captive in a surprise midnight raid, force them to admit to witchcraft and satanism on the Inquisition torture racks, and thus fabricate an excuse to confiscate all their property and lands. Phillip and the Pope both died horrible deaths within the year after the Grand Master, Jacques DeMolay, cursed them as he was burned at the stake for refusing to recant. The nephew of the other Templar Master burned with DeMolay, Geoffrey de Charnay, was the source from which the Savoy dynasty of Italy purchased the Shroud of Turin—the Templar's most sacred relic which preserved the Gnostic truth that the Master Jesus had transmuted his flesh and conquered death.

A huge fleet of Templar ships sailed into the Atlantic immediately before the capture of DeMolay. The Templars had been forewarned, but DeMolay and many others had chosen to remain, trusting in their many political supporters. The Templars received refuge in Portugal and Scotland, and many came to England. They were given special aid by their close associates, the Masonic guilds, whom they had consulted and employed to construct the major cathedrals of Europe. It seems that from this time, Freemasonry became a clandestine vessel for Templar wisdom and tradition. The Masonic Scottish Rite probably preserves synopses of the many different initiatic traditions that had once been synthesized in the Templar Grail or Path of Initiatic Progress.

Recent private research by a leading European Templar indicates the following secret history, which shows that not Larmenius, but a secret succession of Roman Catholic Bishops and Cardinals, actually held and transmitted the Grand Mastership of the Knights Templar under the authority of the Anti-Pope at Avignon after the martyrdom of Jacques DeMolay and papal attempt to destroy the Order. Because Larmenius was chosen by DeMolay, but not elected by an assembly of the Knights Templar, he could not be a valid Supreme Grand Master, like Demolay—although he could transmit Templar tradition and Apostolic lineages.

The persecution of the Templars occurred during the reign of the Avignon Pope in France (there was even a third Pope in Portugal), who competed with the Roman Pope for papal legitimacy. Avignon was a stronghold of Albigensian Gnosticism and the emerging spirituality of the Franciscan Order. It was philosophically and mystically attuned to Templarism. Only the Roman Pope in league with Philip the Fair of France opposed the Templars, and their motives were mainly to confiscate the immense Templar wealth that had accumulated.

After the dangers of the initial persecution of A.D. 1314 had passed, many Templar Knights returned from exile in the Hebrides, most of them arriving in the year 1316. The Avignon Pope clandestinely reinstated the French Templars as the Supreme Order of Christ, officially establishing the new Order in A.D. 1318. It was a cover for the Knights Templar. The same thing was done for the Templars in Portugal, where the Knights of Christ was established as a new religious order under the king's protection. The Knights that had fled to Scotland chose to remain under the protection of the Avignon Pope in France, like the French Templars. Thus, the Roman Pope had no control over them.

On March 25, 1314, in a secret conclave of French Templars at Reims after the martyrdom of Jacques Demolay, a council of Knights Templar had properly elected a secret Supreme Grand Master (*Supreme et Universel Grand* Maitre). This occurred many years before the establishment of the Supreme Order of Christ. Who was this secret Grand Master? He was Jacques D'Euse, Pope John the 22nd—the Avignon Pope himself! According to secret Templar records that we cannot validate, he was known under the clandestine name of Frater Johannes or Johannes P.P. He was succeeded in 1330 by Jacques DeLavie, Cardinal Priest of San Vitale, who was succeeded by another French Cardinal.

We cannot point to any records to verify this secret history, but know the researcher to be a thorough and honest person, highly placed in European Templarism, and with access to records of the Order. It is permitted for us to reveal the facts, but not the source.

In this whole process, then, the Johannite Church was re-established by the Avignon Pope Frater Johannes in 1318, and the Templar Knight Commanders continued to serve as Bishops of the secretly reconstituted Johannite Gnostic Church. This was in deference to the source of Templar Apostolic Orders, which according to the Charter of Larmenius was the non-Byzantine Gnostic Johannite Church of Asia Minor. In Freemasonry the tradition of the "Saints John" is still revered—probably preserving the Templar Johannine tradition in Scotland.

Blavatsky, in *Isis Unveiled*, says that Jesuits of Clermont, wishing to undermine the successful European esoteric orders that were hotly competing with the Church after the French Revolution, fabricated the Larmenius successions to create "dummy" Templar and Martinist orders carefully structured to appear Gnostical, but in reality made to conform to Roman Catholic doctrine in all essential features. If today we carefully examine some of the teachings of supposedly esoteric and Gnostical groups, we will find the truth of Blavatsky's assertions. Richard, Duc de Palatine, emphasized to his students that many so-called esoteric orders are, in fact, mythical restatements of Catholic theology. When we examine the rituals of nineteenth-century non-Masonic Templar orders, we find them to be totally Catholic in theology.

However, we must add that the Larmenius successions of Templar Grand Masters through Portugal (where they were protected) as held by OSMTH seem to be quite genuine, even though they may have been provided by Jesuits plotting to inject "orthodoxy" into Gnostic orders. An examination of these and of the lineage of the Priory of Sion show many evidences of authenticity. There seems also to be evidence that Templar spirituality and Johannite Apostolic Succession was preserved clandestinely within the Roman Catholic hierarchy in France.

It is quite likely that Jesuits did supply the documents for the Charter of Larmenius, but that the documents are historically accurate. The Vatican would have possessed these documents from the sack of the Templars in the fourteenth century, choosing now to make them known for the specific purpose of co-opting the vigorous movement of esoteric Christianity. If so, the Charter of Larmenius is not spurious, and is of great interest and value in reconstructing some of the hidden history of the European Gnosis. This can be seen as having a great infusion through the Knights Templar and the esoteric traditions they absorbed in their Middle Eastern adventures—such as the Johannite Gnostic lineage—then transplanted into European soil as part of the Holy Grail tradition.

From this point forward, Gnosis was practiced and taught secretly as an antidote and corrective to the distortions of Christianity—Catholic, Orthodox, and (eventually) Protestant. Clandestine Gnostic Apostolic Succession was transmitted within the Priory of Sion, the Knights Templar, ever since it was received through the Johannites in the twelfth century.

Clandestine Grail Traditions During the Inquisition

In Europe the suppression of Templarism was followed by a new esoteric impulse that resulted in the circulation of the Rosicrucian Fama, whose descriptions of the Temple of Christian Rosencreutz show some resemblance to the design of von Hohenstaufen's alchemical Castela del Monte. Lord Francis Bacon had been educated in an "academy" whose ideals closely paralleled those of the Pednosophs, who (according to French scholar Michelle Monereau) had now migrated to England to escape persecution on the Continent.

There were by this time communities of Templar emigres in Portugal and Scotland, and is to these latter that the rise of speculative and Scottish masonry are attributed by many scholars, although it is clear that the earliest records of speculative Masonry in London are stamped with Baconian concepts and terminology. In any case, with the Rosicrucian Renaissance of the seventeenth century, the Gnosis began to spread widely through the new vehicle of Freemasonry and it was there that ideas like secular democracy, the brotherhood and latent deity of man, the advocacy of science, the study of non-Christian religion, alchemy, Kabbalah, and ritual magic were carried forth.

Hermetic Science

In the seventeenth century, Ficino translated the Corpus Hermeticum for the last of the Medici's, who wished to see the Teachings before he died. The ensuing impact of the Hermetic Teachings on the intellectual life of Europe was staggering. Within a few generations Pope Alexander VII (the "Borgia" Pope) had become an alchemist and covered his Vatican rooms with magical, talismanic Hermetic paintings. Adepts like Botticelli (Grand Master, Priory of Sion) used Hermetic philosophy to make their images into powerful talismans for the transformation of humanity. Even Catholic orthodoxy was close to accepting the sublime Hermetic philosophy as a way to revitalize the Christian doctrines under the Borgia Pope.

However, a reaction to Hermetic science (more accurately, Hermetic metaphysics) by Catholic counter-reformationists fearful of Gnostic implications for theology, and Protestant Puritan rationalists concerned about black magic, eventually drove the Hermetic impulse underground and into the new English Speculative Freemasonry. Here it later contributed to the Egyptian romances and rites of Cagliostro, Memphis and Mizraim, and Levi's system of magic.

The Illuminist Movement

By the eighteenth century, Freemasonic idealism was creating the conditions for social revolution in England, France, and in the New World. During the last quarter of that century a remarkable adept known as the Compte de St. Germain visited, revitalized, and raised into higher understanding the Masonic and other esoteric lodges of Europe. This was associated with what has been called the Illuminist movement (Martinez de Pasquale, Claude de Saint-Martin, and Martinism; Bavarian Illuminati; Fratres Lucis; and other groups). While many of the French Masonic chapter went to cruel extremes in the Revolution, the Illuminists (with St. Germain) opposed social violence and injustice.

The Compte de St. Germain, who had served as a secret advisor to Marie Antionette by means of anonymous letters since she was very young, was unable to convince the French royal family to take measures that would avoid bloody revolution. He disappeared from European society for several decades after leaving a dire warning about coming events. In the ensuing violence and injustice, many of the Illuminists were beheaded by the extremist Masonic Chapter in Paris as aristocrats and aristocratic sympathizers. The escape of Claude de Saint-Martin from Robespierre's butchers is now considered to be a miracle by many Martinists.

Some of the atrocities of the French Revolution were said to have been perpetuated by members of what have been called the "revenge orders" in Freemasonry. These were the chivalric degrees that were said to have been created by clandestine Knights Templar in Scotland after the martyrdom of DeMolay. In fact, they were idealized and romanticized degrees to memorialize the legacy of the Templars and the injustices of the Pope.

It is likely that members of the Masonic "revenge orders" were greatly responsible for institutionalizing French anti-clericalism during and after the Revolution, as well as for the utopian attempt to design a totally new culture that broke radically from the monarchist past. However, it is extremely unlikely that they would have broken Masonic vows to behead and kill other Freemasons. The Terror was perpetrated by extremists who were denounced by Freemasons of the military orders.

After the Revolution, the Pope, Roman Church, and Inquisitors were no longer in power in France, and for the first time in centuries Gnosticism and underground Templarism were able to emerge publicly. In 1804 Fabre-Palaprat was consecrated Bishop of the *Eglise Johannite des Chretiens Primitifs*, the Johannite Church of the Original Christians, from which came the later French Gnostic churches. He was also installed as Grand Master of the *Ordre Souverain et Militaire du Temple de Jerusalem* and *Ordo Supremus Militaris Templi Hierosolymitani*, the Supreme Military Order of the Temple of Jerusalem (OSMTH), the most authentic order claiming full lineage of descent from Larmenius, to whom DeMolay is said to have entrusted the Grand Mastership when his execution was immanent.

If you examine the T:.H:.G:. lineages of Gnostic Apostolic Succession for which we have extant records, you will find them documented only as far back as Orsini de Gavina (consecrated A.D. 1724). Somewhere there may be records that antedate this by many centuries. However, before this time such records were probably memorized rather than written down for fear of the Inquisition, and they might never be reconstructed. However, what has been documented by Bishop Persson's research demonstrates that the Gnostic Apostolic lineages are known for almost a century before Fabre-Palaprat revealed the existence of the Johannnite Gnostic Ecclesia in France.

The continuation of the Gnostic churches in nineteenth-century France is told in some of the included documents. They veered from their Gnostic orientation after the first half of the nineteenth century, becoming vehicles for the advent of spiritism and spiritualism, or possibly steered off course by Jesuitical infiltration. It appears that these Gnostic churches did not recover their initial Gnostic orientation until the work of Papus and others at the beginning of the twentieth century.

Today the rites of OSMTH, as re-established by Fabre-Palapret (for example), reflect not Gnostic, but purely Catholic ritual and theology. The same seems to have been true of the Gnostic ecclesiae, which by the latter part of the century had fallen into spiritist and spiritualist practices of a most anti-gnostical character and in great need of the kind of corrective forces that came through Blavatsky and the theosophical movement. It was through the efforts of Papus and others that Gnosticism was firmly re-established in the French and English ecclesiae contemporary with the Golden Dawn, O.T.O., John Yarker's Pansophic Rites of Masonry, and the work of Rudolph Steiner.

In England the Order of Corporate Reunion and its antecedents began the process of synthesizing valid Apostolic lineages that were the first time in history, "leaking" out of Catholic and Orthodox churches. The goal of the Order was to create a basis for ecumenical acceptance of Gnosis by the Roman Church.

Today there are two branches of historical Gnostic ecclesiae or churches—the French and the English. Both devolved from the work of Papus and his contemporaries. Other related historical information can be found in *Faivre's Access to Western Esotericism* and in John Yarker's *The Arcane Schools.*

Populist Gnosis

A final note in this overview must be to distinguish the secret, initiatic form of Gnosis received and preserved at the inner core of the Knights Templar from the populist Cathari-Bogomile or Albigensian Christian heresy that was targeted for eradication by Papist armies in medieval Europe.

There were many indigenous Christian Gnostic traditions that flourished independent of Roman Catholicism. The same had been true under the Byzantine Church, where Mandaeans, Pednosophs, and Johannites survived independent of Eastern Orthodoxy as clandestine dynastic orders (i.e., within families from generation to generation). The primary strategy of the Roman Church was to absorb indigenous independent traditions by working out Uniate agreements with them—they would submit to the Pope, but could keep all traditions as long as they were reasonably "orthodox." Even later, as in the case of the Coptic Church, the agreement was for mutual recognition of authorities.

In medieval Bulgaria, the native churches were disrupted by Islamic persecution (ancestors of the modern-day Moslems of Serbia-Croatia). Some chose to convert, but others emigrated to Southern France, where they integrated into indigenous Christian villages. These were the Bogomiles or Albigensians, who kept the memory of their traditions alive through the songs of the Troubadors, the cult of the Virgin Mary (the Magdelene as *Kali*), and in the legends of the Holy Grail.

With Papal approval for appointing a Merovingian king to the politically impotent throne of Jerusalem, the Roman Churchmen thought they had put the genie of heresy into a bottle. The Merovingian successor was now a vassal of the Pope. But through the populist ballads and fairy tales of the Troubadors, the Grail legends, and even by means of the Hermetic art of masters like Botticelli, whose paintings can be understood only in the light of Cathari legends, Gnostic ideals spread throughout European culture.

As in pre-Socratic schools and Hellenistic Gnosticism, where mythology and allegory were used by philosophers to transmit spiritual truth, the medieval Christian Gnostics used the allegories of legend, song, and art to transmit their illicit philosophy. Soon populist Gnosis made common cause with the newly arrived Hermetic philosophy introduced by the translations of Ficcino, and with the new language of Paracelsian medicine, producing Rosicrucian and alchemical romances as well as legends and stories of magical adepts like Shakespeare's Prospero and Dr. Faustus.

However, this populist Gnosis should not be confused with the true Gnostic initiatic orders that were transmitted through clandestine

Johannite Apostolic Succession—at first through the inner circle of Templar chiefs and then, after the attempted extermination of the Order, through secret Templar families who had emigrated to Germany, Portugal, England, and Scotland to escape the Inquisition.

While we lack written records about these secret orders other than the Apostolic Successions from Orsini de Gavina (A.D. 1724) through Royer (A.D. 1800) leading to Fabre-Palaprat and Mauviel, we would not expect anything other than memorized lineages during such an age of persecution. However, it is possible that Vatican archives of the Inquisition carried out by the Dominicans may contain written records or confessions of Gnostic Apostolic Succession from these and earlier times.

In any case, the true initiatic Templar orders of the Grail were lapsing into dormancy by the end of the last century, when in a final effort of fidelity an aged Grand Master managed to perform the Centennial Grail Mass before his order was plundered by the human minions of misanthropic dark forces.

The remarkable events that led to the establishment of the Temple of the Holy Grail in 1988 was a re-awakening of true initiatic Templar orders of the Grail.

Recommended Books (available at www.WesternEsotericBooks.com)

Faivre, A. (1994). *Access to Western Esotericism.* NY: State University of New York Press.

Yarker, J. (1909). *The Arcane Schools.* Privately Republished.

CHAPTER FIVE
THE PRAYER OF THE HEART

"The discussion of prayer is so great a task that it requires the Father to reveal it, His Firstborn Word to teach it, and the Spirit to enable us to think and speak rightly of so great a subject."

Origen

Prayer is the foundation upon which we build our interior Grail Castle. Prayer is the bedrock upon which we sit to practice meditation, contemplation, and other theurgical works. In his book *Jewish Meditation*, Kaplan reminds us, "It is difficult to speak *about* God, but it is very easy to speak *to* God." Speaking to God (prayer) is the first and foundational practice of the Temple and is coordinated with harmonic attunement, alignment, purity practices, and Higher Triad Meditation.

No one outgrows prayer, no matter how advanced in evolution. Saraydarian in *The Psyche and Psychism* writes, "Some of us do not care for prayers, but in esoteric literature we find not only individuals pray, but also Masters pray, and the Ones Who are greater than Masters pray." Alice Bailey, in *Discipleship in the New Age,* writes, "The attitude of the occult student who has thrown over in disgust all old religious practices, and believes one has no further need or use for prayer,…is not a correct one."

As we grow and evolve, the forms and protocols of prayer change. The modes of prayer expand. The expressions of prayer become more universal and beautiful. But there is always prayer in the hearts of all psychic lives, from the least to the greatest. For example, it is said the God of all Gods known prays to the Unknown God, Who in turn offers up prayer, for Divine Life extends into Infinity. This Infinite Divine Life we call

Godhead, El Shaddai, God Most High, Whose Image we are, Whose Presence affirms our existence, and in Whom we move, live, and have our being.

The Evolution and Forms of Prayer

The phenomenon of prayer developed as primal humanity devolved or "fell" through its aeons of development into incarnate expression—or, as the biologist would say, as the animal consciousness of evolutionary predecessors to primates and *homo sapiens* became more self-aware of its separation from its divine origins. Prayer was probably historically what is recapitulated in the ontogeny of every individual—a response to the recognition that one is separated from a primeval bliss faintly remembered in fleeting dreams and flashes of wordless memory. The psychologist relates this to the womb state, but the theosophist relates this to the divine origins of humanity. For both, ontogeny recapitulates phylogeny.

Saraydarian, in *Cosmos in Man*, writes: "At a certain stage in human history a time came when man felt an urge to surpass himself, to stretch himself and touch beyond. This was the unconscious answer of the human being to the conscious call coming from his Soul. As man tried to meet this call he became aware of surrounding obstacles and hindrances, the pain and the suffering, and he began consciously to ask help from an unknown Presence who was near him, but far from his touch. On the path of his struggle he developed a technique of communication which was called prayer. Prayer was performed with an intense desire and aspiration to contact the Presence and ask Its help."

Christian mystics have traditionally employed three methods of interior practice. These are vocal prayer, meditation, and contemplation. Vocal prayer, which can be thought of as talking to God, is probably the most ancient prayer form. It is internal or external conversation that almost anyone can do. Relating to God as the one, true, intimate and real

Person who hears us, and not an abstraction, is the key to the practice of vocal prayer. As Bishop Keizer writes in *The Authentic Jesus*, "…if God is approached with a humble heart and sincere prayer, He-She will respond. The key to prayer is intent, not articulation. One needn't be articulate or facile with words to utter a meaningful prayer. God does not listen to the words, but to the heart." Daskalos, in *The Magus of Strovolos* adds, "Real prayer is not words. By themselves words mean nothing. It is actions and readiness to be of service that count."

In the ancient world, vocal prayer was spoken or formally chanted aloud to a transcendent, king-like Deity. Later, the Master Jesus and others emphasized the power of silent, private prayer to a highly personal, loving God immanent in daily life. Today, we use the more ancient form through Kabbalistic mantra, repetition of powerful harmonic vowels, and techniques of visualization. We integrate the more recent form of private prayer into a consciousness of the sacredness of daily personal life and activities, with practices of contemplation and meditation.

The Development of Personal Prayer

Originally personal vocal prayer, whether in ancient Hebrew religion or in other primitive and shamanic religions, was a crude attempt to manipulate God or the gods by throwing a psychic tantrum. The Hebrew tri-literal root meaning "to pray" means literally "to cut." Ancient Semitic shamans danced themselves dizzy and cut their bodies with a knife to expose the blood. This, (they believed) made their personal will powerful, magical, and persuasive with the gods. Later the ancient prophets dressed in sackcloth and ashes, fasted, danced to exhaustion, and tried to force God's action.

The later Hebrew prophets established another mode of prayer. It was an earnest seeking to know God's will. This also was done by ascetic practices like fasting and prayer, but also with meditation and contemplation.

Jeremiah and prophets of his school divined the Will of God by "hearing" visions, "seeing" the Word of God, and by following inner promptings to do symbolic acts that he would later interpret, such as lying on his left side for so many days in the middle of a busy street. At this point prayer became something far more elevated than an attempt to impose personal will. It became a form of divination and mystic communion with God.

Isaiah achieved something that not even Moses was able to do, for Moses could not see God face to face. To do so would have killed him, we are told. But Isaiah ascended as both priest and prophet to the Throne of God, was purified by a burning coal applied to his lips, and both saw and heard the commandments of the Ancient of Days. From this point forward in Jewish history, a new kind of prayer life and divine communion developed known as Merkabah mysticism, with the beginnings of the oral Kabbalah of the Hebrew master, "great one," or Rabbi (Yiddish Reb).

For at least a century before the time of the Master Jesus, post-prophetic, apocalyptic, and wisdom traditions of Jewish chasidim were developing prayer, sacred meals, and sacred lustrations or washings as forms of priestly "sacrifice" outside of the Temple in Jerusalem. Some of this was in opposition to the non-Zadokite priesthood that had replaced the traditional families of priests in Temple worship, and some was in continuation of the mysticism and practice of the prophetic schools that has traditionally been anti-Temple.

Some of the sects and groups who developed the forms of prayer and ritual that the Master Jesus taught were the various schools of Essenes, the Zadokites, the Damascus and Qumram communities, the Therapeutau, and others on a spectrum from Jewish traditionalists to extremely Hellenized Diaspora Jews. The Master Jesus shared aspects of each of these, but also differed with specific sects like the Essenes and Qumram on many essential points.

St. Paul told of his mystic ascents through the Heavens, and the Gospel traditions chronicled the midnight communion of Jesus with the ascended Jewish masters Moses and Elijah in the narrative of the Transfiguration.

This tradition of divine ascent and communion was continued in medieval and modern Chasidic traditions. The Kabbalistic gateway into this Garden of Paradise, or *Pardes*, became recitation of praise, blessing, and song (psalms). Indeed, the entire canonical Book of Psalms was collected and preserved specifically for priestly and Kabbalistic purposes. It may be compared to both a book of liturgical song and a collection of Jewish mantras. The Psalms were not recited so much for meaning, but for their mantric power. They are still used in this way by Kabbalistic and theurgical practitioners.

Finally, then, prayer was no longer an attempt to impose human will on God, but to *listen and learn from God*. It became what it can be for all contemporary humanity—a basic means of divine communion and reintegration. Prayer as divine communion, both personal and mantric, is taught and practiced in the Temple of the Holy Grail.

Temple Teachings on Prayer

We can begin to understand Temple prayer more clearly by going back and examining what it is not. In our attempts to commune with Heaven we often abuse and distort the relationship. Prayer is not the following:

Prayer Is Not Imposing Personal Will

The ancients tried to force Heaven to serve human will by use of flattery, bribery, appeasement of perceived divine wrath, sacrificial and psycho-magical liturgies, flattering the gods, repetitions of powerful formulas, fasting, and whipping of idols to inflict pain upon the god whose image it reflected. These and many other gimmicks made up the ancient priest-craft that sought omens, wartime assistance, rain, crops, success in the hunt, power over other human wills, success in love, wealth, and the whole repertoire of human desires by means of prayer and associated practices. It has been said by a contemporary comedian that the basic human prayer is: Dear Lord, please break all your Divine Law for my convenience!

Prayer Is Not Simply Telling Heaven One's Personal Need
Heaven already knows one's personal need, but it may not be what the personal self perceives as his or her need. Mother Jennie used to say, Heaven always provides our needs—not our wants!

Prayer Is Not An Atonement For Sin
We cannot talk, beg, or pray our way out of the causes we have generated in life. Rather, we must work out (St. Paul, ergadzomai) our own liberation. One way to facilitate this process is to forgive in prayer. But the person of evil works is not automatically freed from the consequences of such works by mere emotional-mental "conversion." Individuals who have harmed others must not only weep bitter tears, but apply themselves to remedying what they have caused, as far as possible.

Prayer as Esoteric Service and Communion

In the Temple of the Holy Grail, prayer is not primarily a mode of "receiving," but of giving—of sending or qualifying forth seeds, motives, and thoughts. This forms the basis for esoteric service, and later, for the practice of the Blessing Way. In prayer we formulate and send forth or return divine energy ensouling thought, intent, and spiritual action. Prayer is a work, like any other form of communication and articulation.

Prayer, like meditation, must be rhythmic and cumulative. Prayer builds bridges, protective auras, enfolding light, ascending ladders, thought-forms, and higher motivation. The prayers of saints truly aid in upholding the planet from destruction. The "rational sacrifices" of saints work to uplift those who have fallen, and to help make human those who have become depraved. Prayer builds protection, salvation, illumination, world peace, and healing.

Prayer is Divine Creation. The God of the Old Testament prayed when he sent forth the *Fiat Lux*, "Let there be Light," just as the Christian commands, "Let Thy Kingdom (Malkuth) come and Thy Will be done in earth as in Heaven."

Prayer orders chaos, evokes light out of darkness, creates and builds the forms through which the New World can manifest. Prayer sends forth Divine blessing to augment those who heal, serve, and strive to bring forth the New World and the New Humanity, even as water is sent forth by a gardener to strengthen and fructify what he has planted.

Prayer sows the seeds of the future. Prayer works within the powers of time and cosmic currents to sow divine seeds that can bring Paradise back upon earth. The powers of AUM that are taught to Templar Initiates can be used not to insinuate personal will as a black magician, but to cooperate with Heaven by providing a channel to sow the Divine Seed of Shamballa, which is Divine Will that blesses humanity and stimulates higher evolution and transformation. In this sense, prayer is the higher divine work of an Apostle, as St. Peter declares in the Acts of the Apostles.

Prayer is the Bridge over which Divine Revelation and Practice can be brought down into incarnate consciousness. Prayer is one aspect of the Antahkarana—the Rainbow Bridge. Helena Roerich in *AUM*, writes, "Prayer is a conduit to the current of Benefaction."

Kaplan, in *Jewish Meditation*, writes, "How does a person begin to speak to God?" He reminds us that in times of crisis or trouble, prayer is almost automatic. When our lives are running smoothly it is often not as easy for many people. How do we begin? What do we say? Fortunately, we have the prayer of the Master Jesus to guide us.

The Master's Prayer

The Master Jesus considered prayer to be an open gate to infinity. He said, "If you ask, you shall receive; if you knock, it shall be opened unto you." What you receive, and what you find opening up for you, may be quite different than what you had envisioned. But if you accept what is given in answer to prayer with an open heart, you will eventually find that you have been given far more, and far better, than you knew how to ask.

The kind of prayer Master Jesus taught his disciples to use for divine aid and Messianic communion was different than Kabbalistic praise, psalmody, and silent communion—all of which he also taught and used. It was also different from the Jewish Eighteen Benedictions or *Amidah* that was done standing in the Orant position with arms upraised. The model that Jesus taught is found in the extant versions of what has been called the Lord's Prayer. Here the Prayer is rendered in paraphrase by the Grailmaster to emphasize meaning:

Our Father-Mother God in Heaven,
May Thy Way be hallowed in every heart,
Thine Inner Guidance made manifest in every soul,
And thy good Will be done:
As in Heaven, so on earth;
As Above, so below;
As Within, so without;
As in Spirit, so in flesh.

Grant us this day our spiritual sustenance,
And release us from our debts,
As we forgive those in our debt,
Not abandoning us unto the test,
But delivering us from all evil,

Within and without.

For Thine is the Rulership, The Power,
And the Glory forever;

Amen............ Amen.............. Amen

This is an example of the form of personal prayer that was used and taught by the Master Jesus. It is comprised of elements offered in the first person plural ("we," not "I"), with emphasis not upon personal perceived needs, but upon faithfulness to the Divine Way as children under Divine Guidance and Protection.

The Prayer is addressed to our *Abba*, which is an affectionate Aramaic term that a child would use to address his or her "Daddy." The address is not to the *Pater Familias*, but to the Begetter and Generator of all. It is the Kabbalistic concept of God as Progenitor of humanity and all Reality, which proceeds as emanation from the Self-Begotten One. At the heart of each person is the Seed or Divine Spark of God, just as each child originates from the seed of the male parent, as "begetting" was commonly understood in those days. To address Godhead as *Abba* is, in modern terms, to address God in both masculine and feminine qualities as the Divine Progenitor. That is why we specify "Our Father-Mother God."

In Temple Prayer and Meditation these elements include recitations, blessings, and Psalms to draw near unto God (practices of Alignment and Harmonic Attunement), silence to listen to God (Higher Triad Meditation), and in its most extensive form known as the "Vigil," an all-night meditation on a high place far above the "human vibration" for divine communion. For those seeking initiation into the Temple of the Holy Grail, this is done on the Passover Full Moon.

The Master Jesus taught us to address Godhead in silence as one would a revered Elder. He taught us that prayer is private and interior—not something one does publicly or for show. It is said that this prayer alone, if sent forth sincerely and faithfully each day, has power to redeem all humanity.

Higher prayer is always done in the first-person plural. There are several reasons for this. First, none of us is really an "I," but a "we," for we are each holons of holons—a synthesis of many larger psychic lives that are themselves holons of myriad smaller psychic lives. The human soul is a synthesis of untold billions of lives and elements held together in a divine harmony that is ever in danger of disunity and inner disharmony. This harmony becomes ever more unified, beautiful, and perfect as we ascend the spiritual path, but within the complexities of psychic structure are severe dissonances and harmonic flaws that must be transformed by Divine Love in non-self-conscious service to all life, and especially to humanity.

Second, in this process we each gradually assimilate to a greater unity in which the individual human soul is but an element. This greater whole is the spiritual Body for the Perfected Soul of humanity, which is the Christ. The Christ, in turn, is one element in the Body of the Divine Spirit of God, Which is the Lord of Life and has been called Ruah Ha-Qodesh, the Spirit of Holiness or Holy Spirit. Thus every "I" is merely an unrealized "we," and all higher prayer by great initiates is always done in the first-person plural.

In this way the Master showed us that God is like a revered and beloved elder, and must be worshipped in both masculine and feminine aspects. Thus, when we pray to God "in Heaven," we direct our invocation unto the Absolute Ruler and Godhead of all Sacred Rule or Hierarchy, Whose Eyes and Ears (omniscient powers), Hands and Fingers (omnipotent powers) are extended unto us for guidance and help from the Highest Heaven through all intermediary Divine Hierarchy.

To pray for the "highest and best Good" for others is to pray that the Will of God be done in earth—in this *Aeon*, Age, or State of Being—in spite of the disobedience, ignorance, and deafness of humanity to the *Malkuth* or Guiding Rulership of Heaven.

The Way of God is always hallowed, the *Malkuth* of God enforced, and the Will of God obeyed on every level of all Spiritual Hierarchy. Godhead is sovereign over all, and as the Master said, not even a sparrow falls from the sky without the knowledge of our Father-Mother God.

Yet there is what we call "evil" in not only the human world, but in all Hierarchy, because only in Godhead is there perfection. All Hierarchy is becoming more perfect and ascending Godward. But evil is relative, like light. If we hold a match before the disc of the sun, the bright flame appears as a dark shadow. On the surface of the sun we see dark sunspots that, in reality, are so hot and bright that the earth would be turned to a plasma in their environment. Yet they appear dark in relative contrast to hotter parts of the surface.

So it is with good and evil. The "good" in the human world is divine relative to lower systems, but is pale and defective relative to the spiritual hierarchies above. The "good" of the animal world might be expressed in the instinctual killing of weak or sick members of one's own species for the sake of Darwinian survival of the fittest and genetic evolution. But this would be an extreme "evil" for members of the human world, who provide special hospitals and medical aid for human beings who are sick.

In this *Aeon* of flesh, we must look Heavenward for the guidance and sustenance that leads us Godward, because to the invisible angelic hierarchies we are like ignorant children. When we speak of evil, we generally mean "human evil." And yet, to Hierarchy looking down upon our condition, we are to be pitied and helped, rather than condemned for our murders, wars, and crimes. By the same token, however, there are interior and subtle evils lurking within our souls that compassionate Hierarchy might condemn far more harshly than we would. Relative evil depends upon *point of view.*

The point in higher prayer is that the channel to Hierarchy comes through the heart and higher nature of the supplicant. This channels helps build a sensitivity to respond to higher guidance from within.

The advanced disciple is taught by Heaven to align his or her personal will with God's good Will, and then to theurgically manifest what he or she wills as a reflection of Divine Will by channeling spiritual forms into this *Aeon* using occult knowledge that, even if revealed, could not be used by one who was not of high spiritual development. Why could such theurgical techniques not be used successfully by a spiritually unqualified operator? Because he or she would simply lack the interior spiritual and psychical tools to accomplish this kind of work.

Summary of the Teachings of the Master on Prayer

The Master Jesus taught that when we pray, we should:

- pray in private, not in public.

- be sincere and pray from the heart, not for show or other reasons.

- pray in a sense of speaking to one's beloved and respected Parent.

- pray with a sense of humility—not with a sense of superiority to others.

- pray for anything we want because we are children of God. However, there are clear limits. We are not *telling* God what to do; we are merely *asking*. Prayer for the benefit of others in healing, for example, has been demonstrated to be very effective. But what if we pray for our will to be done to others? What if we ask God to convert someone else to our religious opinions? What if we ask God to make us win the lottery? A wise old woman once said, "God answers all prayer, and we must listen and observe to see how God answers us. But God gives us what we *need*, not what we *want*." A good parent does the same.

Esoteric Teachings and Examples of Prayer

In *Temple of the People* of the Halcyon theosophical community under the guidance of Master Hilarion, it is written; "The wisdom of the ages is compressed in the words spoken by Jesus 'Not my will, but thine be done.' It is only prayers preceded by that sentence and winged by an unselfish love, that asks only *to* love, not *for* love, that Omnipotence *can* answer."

Omraam Aivanhov in *A New Earth* taught, "When you wake up in the morning, the very first thing you must do, before anything else, is to give thanks to the Lord." He goes on to offer this advice: "When you want to pray, begin by creating a picture in your mind of a vast multitude of spirits scattered in every corner of the world, each one of which is focused on the LORD. If you unite with these beings and join your prayers to theirs, you will no longer be a lonely voice crying in the wilderness of life; you will be one of thousands of other beings of light who are also calling on Heaven." He also suggested the disciple make the following prayer before sleep; "My God, let me enroll tonight in Your school of love, wisdom, and truth and learn to serve you better, so that Your Kingdom and Your Righteousness may be established on earth."

"Prayer is good at any time, yet there are two periods of change of currents when turning to the Higher World is especially desirable—at sunrise and after sunset. Besides, upon going to sleep it is benefiting to invoke the Higher World." AUM

Amis, in *A Different Christianity* writes, "In the esoteric tradition, prayer is not a child's method of asking for what we want. It is a tool for inner transformation." Atteshlis (known as Daskalos), in *The Esoteric*

Practice, writes: "Prayer comes from the heart. And just as tears born of emotion own a separate chemical composition from those born of physical pain—whether spoken with words or with thoughts—have different vibratory patterns from any other expression. They spring from our deepest nature and seek the ear of the Divine. What is asked for in prayer should be heartfelt, not serving egoism, and dearly desired, for sincere prayer is always heard." Daskalos goes on to write, "Our version of the Lord's Prayer and the complete second stanza have been given to us by the Spirit of Yohannan the Evangelist, an apostle of Joshua. Recitation of the Lord's Prayer, either silently or spoken aloud, is appropriate before beginning any sacred work."

> *Our Father Who Art in Heaven,*
> *Hallowed be Thy Name.*
> *Thy Kingdom come, Thy Will be done,*
> *On earth as it is in Heaven.*
> *Give us this day our daily bread*
> *And forgive us our transgressions as we*
> *forgive those who transgress against us.*
> *And lead us while in temptation*
> *and deliver us from evil,*
> *for Thine is the Kingdom*
> *and the Power and the Glory, Forever.*

> *Absolute Infinite Beingness, God;*
> *Everlasting Life, Love and Mercy;*
> *Manifesting Yourself in Yourself,*
> *as the Total Wisdom and the Almightiness;*
> *Enlighten our minds to understand You as the Truth.*
> *Clean our hearts to reflect Your Love towards You, and*
> *towards all other human beings.*

Here is another example of prayer. This is a gender-free version of the Great Invocation given by Master D.K.

"From the Point of Light Within the Mind of God,
Let Light Stream Forth Into the Minds of All,
Let Light Descend on Earth.

"From the Point of Love Within the Heart of God,
Let Love Stream Forth Into the Hearts of All,
May Christ Return to Earth.

"From the Center Where the Will of God is Known,
Let Purpose Guide Our Little Wills,
The Purpose the Masters Know and Serve.

"From the Center Which We Call the Human Race
Let the Plan of Love and Light Work Out,
And May It Seal the Door Where Evil Dwells.

"Let Light, Love, and Power, Restore the Plan on Earth."

The Grailmaster calls the Great Invocation the first New World Liturgy. It is not the form or specific content that identifies it as such, but the universal energy it qualifies when rightly used. It is intended for public group usage—not as a model for private prayer, although it can be incorporated into private prayer. As group liturgy develops in the coming age, new potent forms of public prayer will be formulated and used for specific purposes and sendings.

One last example is given by Stoutzenberger, in *Celebrating the Sacraments,* who writes: "Anthony de Mello tells a story of a priest who went to visit a sick man in his home. The priest noticed an empty chair at the patient's bedside and asked what it was doing there. The patient said:

'I had placed Jesus on that chair and was talking to him before you arrived...for years I found it difficult to pray until a friend explained to me that prayer was a matter of talking to Jesus. He told me to place an empty chair nearby, to imagine Jesus sitting on that chair, and to speak with him and listen to what he says to me in reply. I've had no difficulty praying ever since.'

"Some days later the daughter of the patient came to the rectory to inform the priest that her father had died. She said: 'I left him alone for a couple of hours. He seemed so peaceful. When I got back to the room I found him dead. I noticed a strange thing, though: his head was resting not on the bed but on a chair that was beside the bed.'"

Serving with Prayer

How can we use prayer to help render useful service? One option is to offer intercessory prayer for those we care deeply about such as our family and friends. We can offer prayer for those people, groups, or countries that come to mind as having a special need. We can also offer prayer for entire categories of people we care about. For example, we can pray for all our Brothers and Sisters in Christ; the New Group of World Servers; all those who comfort the dying; heal the sick; feed the hungry; clothe the naked; shelter the homeless; all those who work for peace, truth, goodness, and beauty; all those who work for the upliftment of humanity; for human rights; for animal rights; all those who work for unity; all those who grieve; all those who are forgotten; all our colleagues. You can also offer prayers for types of human service agencies such as the United Nations, the World Goodwill Organization, the International Red Cross, UNICEF, Childreach, etc. Another option would be to pray for all those with specific kinds of problems. Still another example is to offer prayer for all our Teachers and gurus; for the Masters of Wisdom and Compassion;

for the Blessed One Lord Buddha; the Prophet Muhammad, and for our Eldest Brother, our High Priest, the Master Jesus.

The Arcane School, founded by Alice Bailey, offers this easy-to-use prayer that is now being used by thousands of people all around the world. It is called the noon-time recollection. At noon each day simply lift your thoughts to the Most High and repeat silently or aloud *"I know about the need, oh Lord of Love and Light. Touch my heart that I too may give and love."*

Here is another example of service through prayer also given by the Arcane School. If you decide you want to participate in this service activity, it is suggested this meditation be used once a week, on any day and at any time convenient for you. It is a group meditation even though you may do it by yourself. Many people around the planet are engaged in this meditation and you may join them in Spirit and add to the potency of the eggregore of service.

This service activity should *not* take the place of any regular daily meditation you may already be doing, or the Higher Triad Meditation described in the next chapter, but is offered once a week in addition to your daily practice, and it only takes about 10-15 minutes. It should be a dynamic meditation not brooding or dreamy.

Prayerful Meditation on Service

1. Take a minute or two for alignment and attunement. For now, just imagine that you as a personality are aligned with soul and spirit as an integrated unity. See yourself connected with, and surrounded by, your brothers and sisters in sacred service.

2. Dedicate yourself to the active work of the New Group of World Servers, so cooperating with the Divine Plan.

3. With mindfulness and intensity of thought, say:

*"I am one with the purpose for which the worlds were made.
I am one with the love which animates the Plan.
I am one with the light which streams forth from those who serve the Plan."*

4. Ponder upon those groups and activities in which you serve or of which you are aware. Here you serve by focusing and channeling energy that enlivens, feeds, sustains, and nourishes the eggregore of love-in-action. You think deeply of them, and, in the name of the Christ, imagine surrounding them with Golden Blessings and Goodwill. Give what time you need to this radiation of energy, keeping the mental attitude focused and dynamic. Approach the groups in the following order:

   a.   Your immediate family, home, and business relationships.
   b.   The New Group of World Servers as you may imagine them.
   c.   Finally, into your own immediate field of activity and service.

5. Close by sounding the gender-free version of the Great Invocation as previously given as a means of radiating energy throughout the consciousness of the whole human race.

Daskalos, in *The Esoteric Practice*, provides a wonderful example of how to use communal prayer in service. He writes: "Many want to contribute to the amelioration of the wounds of humanity yet feel helpless. Across the globe there is a network of Researchers who synchronize their prayers for world peace and harmony. You are welcome to join this community. Each day at 9:00 p.m. sit and clear your minds of all thoughts, and fill your heart with unconditional love. If you are a Christian first recite the Lord's Prayer, or should you belong to another faith, recite your own prayers. Envision peace flourishing in the hearts of every man, woman and child in every part of the globe. Sit in peace for a few minutes and then, either internally or aloud, recite this short prayer: *Peace on Earth and goodwill to all. Thy Will be done, on earth as it is Heaven.* There are many time zones and each of us will pray at a particular hour—at 9:00 p.m. local time. It is invaluable to continuously fill this holy and blessed elemental of love and peace with etheric vitality *from* all corners of the globe, *for* all corners of the globe."

Prayer, Gnosis, and Spiritual Integration

It is in prayer that we take the first steps within that lead to divine *Gnosis* or "spiritual knowledge" and the Throne of God. This is an interior knowledge that cannot be taught, but only learned by oneself. *Gnothi Seauton* is the motto inscribed upon the gates of wisdom, said Plato. "Know for Thyself." This is the true *Gnosis Kardia,* the Knowledge of the Heart that must be sought within through prayer, meditation, and works of selflessness. It can be described in discursive teaching like these words here on paper. But it is non-discursive. The spiritual teacher can hope only to awaken a resonance that germinates or potentiates the process of true interior Gnostic development. This sometimes occurs through spontaneous means like taking *darshan* of an awakened being, but it cannot be taught. It can only be attained through the combination of sincere and focused interior search and Grace.

To achieve spiritual integration, we must know ourselves in this entire continuum, from lowest to highest, and we must recognize the child-like status of our normal mundane personal consciousness with its needs and worries. Paradoxically, we must cultivate both profound humility and what in Tibetan Highest Yoga Tantra is called "divine pride." We must know ourselves as both sovereign and servant.

This is accomplished in the form of divine communion we know as prayer, in which we open our hearts as spiritual children and cry for help and guidance to our Divine Parent and all spiritual Hierarchy. Whether it is an Indian shaman fasting and crying for a vision on an isolated mountain top, or a stressed person no longer able to cope without some kind of miraculous intervention, all are leveled and brought into divine communion by sincere prayer.

We pray not as beggars and criminals, but as lost children of *El Elyon*, the Most High One. As lost ones we, like the Prodigal Son, are ultimately servants. As children, we are ultimately sovereigns. In prayer we operate from an acutely focused consciousness between these two polarities.

Closing Comments

Amis, in *A Different Christianity* shares these thoughts about prayer written by Theophan who said: "On first coming to prayer, one should rein in the mind from its distractions and gather it within. One should shake off all cares or quiet them as far as possible, and bring oneself to the most vivid awareness of the omniscient, omnipresent and all seeing God. This creates the inner "closet" or prayer room. It was this which the Lord commanded us to enter in order to pray, a temporary sanctuary. We must be in the inner room or closet. Where is this room? It is in our heart."

Recommended Books (available at www.WesternEsotericBooks.com)

Aivanhov, O. (1992). *A new earth*. USA: Provesta.

Amis, R. (1995). *A different Christianity*. New York: SUNY.

Atteshlis, S. (1994). *The esoteric practice: Christian meditations and exercises*. Cyprus: The Stoa Series.

Bailey, A. (1979). *Discipleship in the new age*. New York: Lucis Publishing Co.

Kaplan, A. (1985). *Jewish meditation.* New York: Shoken Books, Inc.

Keizer, L. (1998). *The authentic Jesus: A guide to Aramaic idioms, recent research, and the original message of Jesus Christ. California:* Privately Published.

Markides. K. (1985). *The Magus of Strovolos.* New York: Penguin Books.

Roerich, H. (1980). *AUM.* New York: Agni Yoga Society, Inc.

Saraydarian, T. (1973). *Cosmos in man.* Arizona: Aquarian Educational Group.

Saraydarian, T. (1981). *The psyche and psychism,* volume two. Arizona: Aquarian Educational Group. Temple. (1948). *Teachings of the temple.* California: The Temple of the People.

CHAPTER SIX
THE CUP OF LIGHT

Introduction to Higher Triad Meditation

The individual, incarnate human ego is like a royal prince or princess who has forgotten their origin and "knoweth not whence they came and whither thcy goeth." Yet he or she is the royal heir to the Kingdom.

The Quest Begins

When finally one has plumbed the depths of duality and filled oneself with the "husks" of illusion, one begins to glimpse a memory of who and what one truly is. The veil between God and humanity is partially rent, and one begins to yearn for his or her true Home. The individual then undertakes the Divine Quest that leads—precept upon precept, degree by degree—along the homeward journey. This is the theme of such classic parables as the Gnostic *Hymn of the Pearl* and the *Prodigal Son* of Master Jesus.

For each of us, it is the work of making Pinocchio into a "real boy," (or girl) for which the absolute and whole-hearted cooperation of Pinocchio is vitally necessary. We should have no illusions that Pinocchio will become "real" in any way but step upon step, precept upon precept, experience and failure by experience and success! This is the "natural way" of the Divine Embryo that lives within us, and it is the basic process through which the Single Eye and all other psycho-noetic senses will unfold us.

What is the "natural way"? It is the deep work of human service done in the light of prayer and meditation. It means fully engaging humanity, nature, and one's own human nature in the alchemical retort of daily, perseverant contribution to the Great Work of Hierarchy.

In the Temple of the Holy Grail, the ancient mysteries are being reconstructed in vital forms to help and guide those ready to receive what we call the invisible *Sang Real* or Royal Blood that comes to us like a new hormone released into the systems of pubescent humanity, facilitating the amazing change from youth to adulthood.

The main techniques we employ in traveling this initiatic journey include study, prayer, harmonic attunement, purity practices, service, meditation, Initiation, and Empowerment. This chapter lays the metaphysical foundation for meditation and presents some of the many benefits and results of carrying out a lifetime practice. In the following chapter we provide detailed instructions for beginning your daily practice of Higher Triad Meditation.

What is Meditation?

Meditation is an approach to self-knowledge that uses direct subjective experience as a means of revealing and integrating untapped creative, intuitive, and psychic faculties. It includes techniques that are effective in amplifying and fine-tuning existing abilities or skills as well as methods for psychological self-discovery, analysis, and positive transformation. Thus meditation is a kind of 'high tech' approach to the systematic unfoldment of human potential.

Meditation is a daily practice that produces long-term, cumulative effects. Over the years, meditation can result in deepenings, maturations, ripenings, and sequential unfoldments of expanded awareness and self-mastery in mental, emotional, and even physical life. Advanced meditators often develop and can demonstrate conscious control over basic cellular functions of their own physical bodies.

Meditation is not a religion or set of beliefs, although meditative, contemplative, and related mystical and spiritual practices have been carried into modern times through the cultural traditions of religion. Meditation is a tool of consciousness that allows us to work dynamically with direct experience of relatively uncharted human potential that in ancient times was attributed only to gods, and it clears the way for the evolution of a wiser, more expanded human nature not only among individual practitioners, but in all human society.

From the treasury of meditation paths and practices that developed among historical religious, yogic, and shamanic traditions, it is possible to discover, expand, and adapt techniques for modern people that can develop into fruitful daily practice. Although it is desirable for a meditator to seek and find a skilled teacher who can guide him or her through effective traditional practice, it is also possible for many to follow an intuitive, more interior guidance that draws from readings and encounters with many different teachers and schools.

There is no reason to be intimidated by all the schools, paths, and variations of meditation practice. The countless varieties of meditation techniques are simply "skillful means" of integrating increasingly better, more inclusive, more sensitive, and more refined maturations of expanded consciousness (or ego-state, or self-awareness) into conscious, daily life and personality. The choice of technique, or of school, or of teacher (if necessary), is not of primary concern in order to begin a fruitful daily practice. These things may or may not be useful at a later time, as meditation begins to be established in one's life.

In the Temple of the Holy Grail we practice the Higher Triad, White Light, or Iliaster Meditation. Higher Triad Meditation, used in conjunction with Temple Purity Practices, Prayer, and Harmonic Attunement, serves as a high-tech approach to the systematic unfoldment of human potential.

Temple meditation also serves as an occult daily practice for optimizing and making fully conscious the inevitable process of physical death, whenever it comes. We develop the ability to fix attention upon the White Light and ignore all other manifestations, as practiced in ancient Egyptian, medieval Hermetic, Tibetan Buddhist, and other advanced yogas for the art of dying. Remaining fixed upon the Holy White Light while our body dies will be our final incarnate work to achieve continuity of consciousness. It can produce profound results beyond the scope of this simple introduction.

The Necessity of Meditation

Meditation is a necessary tool for people serious about individual and planetary spiritual attainment. Meditation is a world service, like prayer, requiring self-discipline, commitment, and perseverance. Even the advanced disciples of Master Jesus found it a hard practice, but it is necessary for the unfoldment of the New World and the New Humanity.

After a certain point of unfoldment, without meditation there is no progress. It is always difficult to begin the discipline of meditation. It's like learning to read. Few people would bother to learn were it not for teachers, parents, and social goals. But once they take the trouble to learn, their entire life is unimaginably enriched, broadened, and filled with potentialities impossible for those who are illiterate.

To those accustomed to meditation, it becomes the sweetest part of the day. But to those who complain that they are no good at it and they find it too difficult, it seems strange that anyone could enjoy meditation!

Meditation is an approach to Self Knowledge. It is a high-tech method of systematic unfoldment of human potential. It must be a daily practice or it doesn't work. It produces long-term cumulative results. Over the years it produces ripenings, deepenings, maturations, sequential unfoldings of expanded awareness, higher ego states, and self-mastery.

Brief Historical Background of Western Meditation

The Master Jesus taught a Semitic form of meditation that had been used by prophets from the time of Moses. Christians sometimes call it the Vigil. There are many descriptions of the Vigil in the New Testament. When Jesus is quoted in the New Testament as exhorting his disciples to "watch," he is using the Aramaic word for vigil, or meditation.

Master Jesus took his closest disciples to a quiet wilderness, usually upon a hilltop or mountain, and they spent the night in Vigil. It was during such a Vigil that Peter and the others had their eyes opened and saw the Master speaking with Moses and Elijah, advanced members of Hierarchy. They also saw Jesus transfigured in his glory as a spiritual being—a sight normally hidden to their eyes of flesh.

Why was the vigil carried out at night? It is likely that the Master kept Vigil at night-time for several reasons. First, it is then that most of humanity in the area sleeps, physical and mental commerce ceases, and space is far less disturbed. The lower human vibration wanes and meditative clarity is more possible. Second, darkness removes physical sense stimulation, which stands like a wall between lower and higher consciousness. He chose hilltops and mountain tops because lower human mental vibration tends to seek a lowest level, like water, and collects in the plains and valleys.

The major problem the disciples had was staying awake during the Vigil. Once they dozed off, they lost continuity of consciousness and could just as well have been in bed. Master Jesus exhorted them to keep awake and in a state of prayer—that is, in a special, private, interior state of communion with Heaven—a Eucharistic heart-prayer. That is, rather than repetition of mantras, they spoke in a personal manner to Heaven. Even when repeating psalms they personalized each word. This magnetized what in Egypt was called "returning grace," thanksgiving, or Eucharist, for it reflected Divine Energy back to its source, thus purifying the channel. This tradition was carried on by the apostles and later resulted in desert monasticism and the mystic practices of Christianity.

In the *Testaments of the Twelve Patriarchs*, mystic Pharisaic revelations of the centuries before Jesus that contain much of the content of the Christian Sermon on the Mount, high Vigil is called the Trance of Death. This is because meditation enters the same consciousness as the death-state. Meditation seeks pure consciousness apart from the physical body, except maintaining the thread of conscious continuity that allows higher revelation to descend into lower or "conscious" mental activity. This bringing of Heaven down into earth and incarnating the higher into the lower is a variation on the traditions of Kabbalistic ascent to the Throne-Chariot or Merkabah of God. It was practiced by Jewish mystics of the Second Temple and by early Christians like Paul, who tells of his ascent to the Third Heaven of Paradise. Later esoteric and mystic Christianity perpetuated such techniques of divine meditation and contemplation.

It is common to distinguish between Eastern and Western methods of meditation but a better distinction might be Yogic and Shamanic, since both forms existed in East and West and even within the vast traditions of Buddhism and Christianity. Jesus used Shamanic techniques native to Jewish prophetic and Semitic spirituality, as did Mohammed.

Contemporary discipleship makes use of both Eastern and Western meditative technique, but technique is not the essence of meditation. Technique becomes a matter of individual preference—if it works, use it!

Higher Triad Iliaster Meditation

What is the Higher Triad? The Higher Triad is a term for the union of the Heart, Throat, Ajna, and Crown Chakras, which form a specific psychic entity. A single-pointed meditation focus linking the consciousness of heart and mind, as taught by the Master Jesus and in Temple practice, is a Higher Triad meditation.

What is the Iliaster? The Iliaster is the primordial and limitless Light of God, the Gnostic *Nous* or Kabbalistic *Ain Soph Aur* that constitutes the primal emanated manifestation of Godhead. It is known in Tibetan Buddhism as *Rigpa* or the crystalline Mind of pure Reality. The Iliaster is also called the Holy White Light of Christ. It is the Creative Light of Godhead that sleeps within our Hearts.

This Holy White Light exists in four gradations of sublimity, according to the teachings of Paracelsus and the alchemists. It is the basic and essential "stuff" out of which all manifestation occurs, and out of which all subtle creative work may be done. We must be able to evoke, sense, and to be in touch with the Iliaster in order to do any kind of mantic or magical work.

The First or most sensible form of the Iliaster is a white, milky Light we evoke for practices of the Blessing Way, liturgical work, healing, and for successful completion of Temple Empowerments. Higher Triad Meditation is designed to facilitate our ability to evoke direct contact with this Holy White light of Christ, which is sensed subjectively as gentle gathering clouds of subtle white Light during Temple meditation.

Our meditation technique is a "single pointed awakening" similar to what the Master Jesus taught his disciples, whom he constantly reminded to remain awake during the Vigil. There are indications that the Knights Templar and other mystics of their era practiced the White Light Meditation. The method was used extensively by Christian and Gnostic quietists of the period as well as Kabbalists. Such mystics as Matthew of Aquasparta, St. Bonaventure, and John Peckham, Archbishop of Canterbury, advocated that "certainty was attainable through direct contact with the Divine uncreated Light."

Temple meditation is a form of *communion and attunement* with Higher Guidance accomplished by "Vigiling" or "Watching"—i.e., by means of single-pointed meditation focused upon seeking higher vision and audition. The meditator is awake and alert, looking and listening for divine guidance, not unlike the American Indian brave, who went alone to a mountain top "crying for a vision."

It is working with the Divine Energy Itself, face-to-face. It produces what has been called "straight knowledge" or intuitive Gnosis. It becomes a means to achieve instant sacred communion with Divine Reality. It is breaking through veils of lower personal ego states to see and view from Higher Ego states—the One Heart, the One Being, WE. It is a method for expanding the "I" into "We." This method of Higher Triad Meditation will be fully explained in the next chapter.

Rending the Veil

The first result of persistent daily meditation (usually after a minimum of several months) is to penetrate and break through the ground or veil of limited consciousness into what could be called a vast and luminous nectar of awakened consciousness. At first this breakthrough occurs only for a second or two. Subjectively, it feels like falling asleep because one can't hold the energy and bring it back. But it's not falling asleep. It's a falling awake!

When that happens you will suddenly come back to self-awareness and think something like, "Oh, I was in a place of Great Light, Great Peace, Great Harmony!" Once you have established that contact, the veil of the Temple has been rent and it's now easier to enter the Sanctuary of Light. From that point on, you should do the meditation persistently each day *until you achieve the state of Light*—if only for a second or two. Eventually you will be able to widen the rend in the veil and remain in the state of Light for more extended periods.

The whole goal of this type of meditation is to achieve the Light and then hold yourself in that state. It's not a state of brilliant flashing lights. It's a state of soft clouds of illumination. It's a vast state because the consciousness is extremely expanded. You are sitting in a position of great awakedness and real awareness with great calm. It has been called luminous or enlightened because there is no longer a sense of void or darkness or emptiness. You realize, understand, experience, and *know* that there is no void, there is no space that is not luminous, that everything is filled with a kind of light. It is an experience of light but a gentle kind of light. Disciples of the Master Jesus call it the "Holy White Light of Christ." It is likened to a nectar because it feels very sweet, like mother's milk to an infant.

Meditation Helps Prepare for Daily Living

Going into the state of Light before beginning the work of the day offers tremendous benefits. As you step out into the struggles of daily life, you find yourself in a state of much higher attunement and intelligence than has been normal for you. You keep a cooler head and are able to function more effectively and realistically, able to concentrate and focus effort, visualize solutions to problems, to think on your feet, tap into intuition and spontaneous helpful insights, to approach emotional problems and conflicts with less static and worry.

As you begin to develop the new, higher ego-state that you now carry into daily life from this place of Light, your other mental faculties begin to function "in the moment," spontaneously, with expanded awareness. This effect might be described as a gain in intelligence and mental, emotional, and even physical self-mastery.

Everything that a meditator achieves in meditation is a permanent asset. It isn't something that ends or something that can be lost. What you gain is always with you. What you gain is an asset that becomes part of what is called the "Chalice," which is that center of your energy from your heart center that contains and accumulates non-verbal, non-three-dimensional, non-material essences, nectars, and fragrances that are carried from lifetime to lifetime. Every achievement made in meditation, every achievement of drawing closer to a conscious awareness of higher realities, and the higher worlds, every attainment that is made in attuning oneself is a permanent building of the Antahkarana, the Rainbow Bridge.

This is an interior kind of growth which activates and brings what was hitherto unconscious into a field of expanded consciousness. Although you may develop, "ripen," or complete and then leave some kind of specific practice or specific achievement, the effects it produced remain as a foundation or building block for more advanced work.

You may begin to become aware of living and looking out in to the world from a higher, more advanced ego-state, which at first is the ego-state of "we." It's the ego-state of compassion being able to feel the pain of others and feel or see from the point of view of the other person in a clearer way than ever before, in such a way that it becomes impossible to hate, or to desire to do harm to anyone. The love petals of your lotus begin to unfold. As this occurs and the definition of self becomes more expanded, you eventually begin to make clear contact with higher guidance that comes through intuitive flashes—straight knowledge, direct knowing.

As you are able to identify with and integrate successively higher ego-states towards the One Great Self, "Thou Art We, We Art Thou, Thou Art I, I am Thou," then your meditation itself becomes continual. That is, the state of Light has been awakened and radiates from your Heart at all times, though in fluctuations from low to high intensity depending up many other things.

You begin to achieve meditation states with your eyes open, on your feet, and as you go through your day. As you are able to integrate this higher reality and these higher ego-states, this becomes more your normal frame of perception. As the Master Jesus said, "The Sabbath is not one day a week, it's every day of the week; all times are sacred, and all places are sacred."

One day you will take your place as a co-worker with the One Self and enter into intimate dialogue with the treasury of esoteric Reality. You will begin to be brought into greater spheres of work for the benefit of all beings. You will be able to empathize with all beings as "self." You will make telepathic and even physical contact with other highly developed brothers and sisters who are doing similar but coordinated kinds of work under the same higher planetary guidance—the work of the Elders and the Great Plan, and the Hierarchy, selflessly promoting the higher evolution of human consciousness in the various fields of human activity.

How do you develop this sacred alchemy of meditation? *You just have to do it, and do it, and keep doing it*—and eventually you begin to hit pay dirt. Meditation becomes a sweet thing that you look forward to every morning. But if you don't do it regularly, rhythmically, and devotedly, you will have little or no result.

There are many human beings world-wide who quietly function at "superhuman" levels. They do not reveal themselves under most conditions, and they do not offer their wisdom or guidance on the market places or in books. Many of them no longer inhabit remote mountains, but live near population centers. Through the Holy Light, you will be brought into their company if you make the private and individual effort necessary. Temple practices are designed to optimize your efforts.

Meditation Helps Unlock our Higher Nature

Meditation sets us on an undistorted course each day if we devote five to fifteen minutes upon arising. We start out harmonized and attuned. As the day progresses we try to keep in touch with that morning contact with the Higher Nature. We can meditate anywhere and any time once we develop our own working technique. Combined with self-forgetful service, meditation and prayer, we begin to unlock our Higher Nature. The Divine Seed germinates and sprouts within our hearts. We begin to sense and know things previously hidden to us. Higher octaves of sensation, consciousness, and perception open to us. The Love and Knowledge Petals of the Lotus unfold, and we find our spheres of service expanding, our spiritual responsibilities increasing. We grow and create in ways we never before envisioned.

Meditation Leads to Enrichment of Life

As one gains interior harmony, life becomes better, richer, and more easily mastered. One becomes creative in many areas instead of perhaps one. The "Renaissance Person" is one who holds Higher Communion. All sensation becomes multi-dimensional. Food tastes better. Great solemnity, joy, and wisdom can be perceived in nature. True selfless love begins to flavor and color sexuality, parenting, human relations. One is more awake, more alive, more present here and now, more creative, more intelligent, more competent. One is able to discover the wisdom of life without books and teachers. One lives progressing ever unto the Divine Heart, seeing behind effects into causes.

Meditation Leads to Higher Communion

Meditation is a collective activity, even when sitting alone in silence, for space is filled with life, and Higher Life meditates continuously. Meditation simply means being in communion with the Higher. One's morning meditation becomes a touchstone for continuous daily communion in work and play.

In meditation we experience *kenosis*, the emptying of personal self and filling of Higher Self. This makes us more beautiful, more loving, more inspired and inspiring—more fiery. We replace the little self with the Higher Nature, and renounce so-called "free will" in order to reflect Higher or Divine Will. Instead of seeing ourselves as the focal center around which the universe revolves, we begin to recognize our key on the piano, our string on the harp, our place in the grander scheme, and this makes us more effective, more efficient, more able to develop fully as a realized individual.

Meditation Builds the Rainbow Bridge

Meditation builds the *antahkarana* or psychic bridge between our four occult bodies and the higher planes of Reality. Thus, it builds continuity of consciousness. Through meditation we can eventually become lucid dreamers, able to be "awake" in our sleep and consciously participate in the Great Work of Hierarchy. We may become more aware of our psychic interconnection with all life and discover we are able to make practical, applied use of intuition and hunches in our life work. We can find ways to harmonize our daily work with the Great Work, and start to become co-workers with Hierarchy, advancing in Initiation and human service.

Meditation Helps in the Preparation for Higher Life

Meditation is preparation for the death-state, which is life and consciousness unlimited by physical form, yet limited by unfoldment of consciousness. It is the very practice we will need to achieve continuity of consciousness during physical death. Meditation moves us out of the hells of life and death because it builds Nobility, Calmness, Justice, Love, and Joy within us. Meditation gives us resources to meet the crises of life—to overcome fear, anger, failure, depression. It is through meditation that we receive "spiritual sustenance," as described in the Master's Prayer.

What Meditation is Not

Meditation is not a means of becoming superior to other souls. Weed out any such motives. Meditation is not a means to earthly power. It is a commitment to spiritual self-forgetful service. Meditation is not mere astral wandering or dozing. Such a practice in the name of meditation is as dangerous as use of psychedelic drugs. Meditation need not be long and painful. Five minutes every morning after prayer, attunement and alignment is fine. The important thing is regularity and rhythm—not length. Meditation is not just affirmations and visualizations. Meditation is not gimmicks. It is wordless striving of the heart that *may* use mental forms as vehicles. But they are not the essence.

Motives for Meditation

The ancient Merkabah mystics of Palestine were well aware of the consequences of wrong meditation. We find in their writings, as in the monuments of many of the world's mystic traditions, strong warnings against mystical practice by those whose motives were impure. The Tibetan Buddhists emphasize *boddhichita*, or pure spiritual motivation to work for the benefit of all beings, as primary and foremost in any practices for spiritual self-evolution. The American Indians did their work "that my people may live." This *must* be your motivation for Temple work. Be very certain that you begin, continue, and end in that motivation.

Impure motivation—desire for spiritual superiority, power over other wills, social or religious power and leadership, psychic power—all these create conditions that lead to highly undesirable consequences. We all have these impurities, so we must "crucify" them by making ourselves aware of them. Not by browbeating ourselves, but simply by allowing ourselves to acknowledge them and make them naked to our eyes. That is all it takes to begin to master them.

We develop this simple technique of purification in our first work of the Empowerment Over Darkness, or First Empowerment. It is known as the Necklace Practice.

Serious meditation can begin while one still has these weeds in the garden of the soul, but only if one is committed to remove all vestiges of them. None of us is without ego and selfish desire. If we all waited until we felt we were perfect, we would be deluded! It is imperative to be aware that such seeds and weeds exist within, because only then can we recognize the signs of their manifestation and learn to guard against them in our practices and works.

Know Thyself! First, get a good idea of faults, separative desires, and other egoistic tendencies. Then, knowing the Inner Enemy, proceed on the Path. We use various ways and means that will be introduced in later chapters on Temple Purity Practices. As a preview, some of these Purity Practices include: the evening review, prayer, contemplation, use of sacred oils, imperil elimination, and work done when completing certain Empowerments.

Purity begins by recognizing one's own impurity. Anyone who claims to already be pure is ignorant of himself or herself. But ultimately, impurity does not exist within the Heart—only the things that nurture impurity. Impurity, when hosted by the Heart, can eventually result in defilement, which does proceed from the Heart, just as suicide proceeds from the inverted will of a living being.

The Importance of Regularity and Perseverance

Just as a musician cannot become a great performer unless he or she invests hours of regular, faithful daily practice on the instrument, so a neophyte cannot develop towards initiation without regular, rhythmic, perseverant spiritual practice. Unlike a musical instrument, the instrument of the probationer is internal. It is the mind, heart, soul, and character of the probationer that must be focalized, exercised, and trained in daily practice.

The best time to begin meditation is immediately after awakening, before the mind has been stimulated. But when you have developed results, you may find other times that are good for meditation.

Often the most enduring results are achieved when meditation seems most difficult—when there is external distraction, psychic attack, social pressure, or a lack of any motivation to sit and do your practice. Under those conditions you can make far more progress than when everything comes easily and fluently—*if you persevere and make your best effort to focus, concentrate, and achieve the goals of the practice sincerely and wholeheartedly.* But if you merely go through the motions of practice, very little is achieved. It is important to do each practice with full presence.

Daily Practice

Each daily practice consists of several parts. The first might be called prayer, but it is really a process of interior striving—uplifting your mind and heart for attunement with Divine Reality. It is a process of contacting your own central point of "stillness," or what is known in Buddhism as "calm abiding," and opening yourself to greater spiritual communion and the experience of inner light. It begins with prayer in words, but ends in silence.

The second part is one of the two aspects of that same communion with Divine Reality. In the morning we *meditate* because the mind is relatively quiet, having recently awakened from sleep. Meditation is a non-verbal or non-discursive abiding in expanded consciousness through a focus—in the case of Temple Meditation, a focus on Holy White Light.

Each night, just before falling asleep, we *contemplate* through use of an evening review. The goal of this contemplation is to objectively review our daily activities in reverse order. It is non-judgmental. It only requires 3-4 minutes and is done for the purpose of evaluating what and how we have performed spiritually throughout the day. This evening review helps builds the antahkarana and encourages development of continuity of consciousness.

The daily practices must be regular and rhythmic because each day a small gain is achieved, but it is diminished or lost by each day of neglect. So theoretically if we practice only every other day, we would have a net progress close to zero. However, even if we practice poorly, but do it regularly, we would make some progress. How much more if we practice regularly and try to make each session perfect!

This is not to say that spiritual practices perfect the souls of humanity! What perfects the soul of each person is his or her response to the tests and trials experienced in the furnaces and fires of daily life. How does one deal with an enemy? How does one handle a terrible loss?

Spirituality builds a greater soul that is able to bear more sorrow and hold more joy than is possible for ordinary souls. Each of us experiences a time and a season for everything, positive and negative. But though we may be forced to drink even more bitter dregs than we think we can bear, we are also able to sip a far sweeter and more fragrant wine than those who have not yet awakened to the life of Spirit.

So persist in daily practice, and bring into your daily life the tools, powers, energies, and equipment that daily spiritual practice develops in you. Only in this way can you make progress toward initiation.

Remember, with a determination to be punctual and regular in meditation and prayer, it is easiest to carry out the practice upon awakening or before retiring. The best practice is to pray and meditate upon awakening and before eating, making telephone calls, or otherwise being drawn into worldly work—just as it is better to tune the violin before the concert than after it!

When retiring for sleep, meditation, prayer, or reading of spiritual books is the best way to prepare consciousness for sleep, which is every bit as active and conscious as daily work but hidden from most minds—just as it is good to prepare oneself for death as it approaches, if possible. The level of consciousness before sleep or death determines one's "starting place" in any ascent to Higher Reality—which is a matter of pure consciousness. Finally, pray for help and guidance in meditation.

One may find it easier to meditate with a group in order to get a "feel" for techniques and goals, and then take this experience into private daily meditation. One may wish to link with an advanced meditator or teacher at first to help balance his or her efforts. One may work in a Triangle or with a spouse. But ultimately your meditation is your own.

From now on unto infinite Eternity, you will be a meditator. You will be in Holy Communion. You will meet and come to know your co-workers, who are advanced disciples and members of Hierarchy. You will know increasing individuality, joy, wisdom, Light. You will evolve, expand, grow, and serve.

The next chapter provides detailed instructions for beginning your daily practice of Higher Triad Meditation.

Recommended Books (available at www.WesternEsotericBooks.com)

Atteshlis, S. (1994). *The esoteric practice: Christian meditations and exercises.* Strovolos: Cyprus: The Stoa Series.

Bailey, A. (1979). *Letters on occult meditation.* New York: Lucis Publishing Company.

Kaplan, A. (1978). *Meditation and the Bible.* Maine: Samuel Weiser.

Kaplan, A. (1985). *Jewish meditation.* New York: Schoken Books.

Kaplan, A. (1995). *Meditation and Kabbalah.* London: Jason Aronson.

Saraydarian, T. (1971). *The science of meditation.* California: Aquarian Educational Group.

CHAPTER SEVEN
DAILY PRACTICE OF
HIGHER TRIAD
MEDITATION

M any people want to begin or deepen their meditation practice but feel unsuccessful when they try. Their mind wanders, they don't feel any benefit from what they are doing, and often wonder whether they are doing things "right." When they don't find the cosmic bliss they have been led to expect, they often end up feeling discouraged. This chapter—a distillation of centuries-old wisdom from many traditions—can help the serious practitioner move into a productive daily practice of meditation. It should be read and re-read several times.

View

If a person develops a long-tem view and realistic expectations about meditation, and follows an effective daily practice based upon an analysis of his or her particular mental tendencies, then after many months of commitment and perseverance, he or she will often begin to enter a process of "break-through" into a luminous nectar-ocean of ever-expanding awareness.

This "break-through" then becomes the foundation for additional "learnings" and serves as the basis for all further progress. The meditator enters, degree-by-degree, into intimate dialogue with the treasury and profundity of subtle, invisible, esoteric reality hidden from normal minds and works for the greater good of all other beings.

Ultimately, one begins to achieve these states with eyes open, on one's feet, and as you go through your day. As the Master Jesus said, "The Sabbath is not one day a week, it's every day of the week and all times are sacred and all places are sacred."

How to Begin

The first approach to meditation is to simply sit and focus in order to discover how your particular mind operates to distract you and keep you boxed into normal mental consciousness. There are many time-honored techniques for this, but we suggest sitting in three sessions on separate days for a period of five to ten minutes to do the following sequence of three exercises—one each day in the order given.

To help you maximize your results, here are some suggestions you can use that others have found helpful. These instructions, which concern creating a sacred meditation place and meditation posture, will apply both to your three-day exercise and your on-going, daily practice of Higher Triad Meditation.

Creating a Sacred Space for Meditation and Other Spiritual Work

It is strongly suggested that you create a special and private meditation place. Ideally this would be a room used exclusively for your spiritual work but it could also be a dedicated corner of your bedroom. This space will eventually become "saturated" with elementals created by your spiritual aspirations and intent, thus making it easier for you to enter into the state of consciousness associated with the Divine Iliaster. Elementals can be thought of as living entities constructed of etheric and noetic substance. They are created by the interaction of human thought and desire.

Elementals are life-forms created by thought, fueled by desire, whose function is to achieve some type of fulfillment.

• Designate a chair or cushion for meditation that no one else is allowed to use.

• Psychically cleanse your cushion or chair using a little eucalyptus or sandalwood oil diluted in water and sprinkled, (or as incense with the smoke wafted into the fabric).

• Consecrate your chair for your exclusive use by placing your left hand over your heart, and extending your right hand towards the object. With clear intent to purify this object, chant one OM while simultaneously visualizing a violet light radiating all around this chair or object burning away all impurities and leaving it psychically cleansed. Then chant one more OM while simultaneously imagining your meditation chair or cushion surrounded by and saturated with the blessing of golden light.

• Set up an altar of sacred objects as they come to you and keep it in your meditation spot. In the beginning you may have only one or even no objects.

Meditation Posture

• In your own sacred place where you are free from interruption, free from physical distraction, and free from discomfort, sit comfortably in a chair with your feet on the floor and with the spine perpendicular to the ground (not slouching or held in an artificially stiff position).

- Relax your body completely. Unless you are used to sitting in yogic postures comfortably, it is best to either sit in a chair, or to use some sort of high cushion or cushion-and-box combination. To keep the body happy, the knees should be lower than the hips. Comfort is vital to assure that the physical body doesn't become a distracting battleground of aches and itches.

- Rest the hands comfortably with palms facing up, on your knees or thighs, with the tips of the thumbs touching the tips of the forefingers.

- Your head should be tilted slightly down (too far down will cause drowsiness), with the eyes gently closed, positioned straight ahead, and facing a window or other source of slight illumination. We do not recommend sitting in darkness because it tends to promote drowsiness. We also do not recommend using a candle light alone because the flicker of the flame tends to distract.

- If possible, face East when you meditate. If you can, wear a white meditation garment (cleansed and consecrated) used only for this purpose.

Preparation for the First Day's Exercise

Even though it is not necessary, you may want to begin these three day's of exercises at the first convenient time after the exact time of the New Moon. Aivanhov, in *The Book of Divine Magic* writes; "Whenever you want to undertake something new, to carry out or, alternatively, to put an end to a project of some kind, you will always get better results if you know how to use the influence of the moon. If you have to inaugurate some important work or activity…it is more likely to succeed if you wait until the waxing moon…"

You can find out when the exact time of the New Moon is by consulting a local newspaper or the Old Farmer's Almanac. You may also wish to ask or pray for Divine or Higher Guidance that by completing these initial exercises you will gain an understanding of which types of distractions most effectively impede you during meditation—whether they are visual, auditory, or tactile.

For best results, complete the following three exercises on separate days before proceeding with the Higher Triad Meditation.

The First Day's Exercise

Remember, the goal is to discover which types of distractions you are most prone to.

1. Sit in the meditation posture as previously described, take a few deep breaths, and then relax. With eyes closed, focus your attention onto the tip of your nose and begin to "watch" your breaths. Inhale and exhale slowly through your nostrils, and count each cycle of breath as it comes and goes: 1…2…3…Don't allow your mind to wander or be distracted by anything. Simply stay on task counting breaths. When you lose count, start again from the number one. Do this for about five minutes.

2. When you finish, write on a sheet of paper how many breaths you were able to take before losing count, and record what things seemed to be distracting you—sounds, thoughts, worries, uncomfortable physical sensations, etc. It is vital that you remember and record everything you can remember about your distractions.

The Second Day's Exercise

Remember, the goal is to discover which types of distractions you are most prone to.

1. Sit comfortably in the meditation posture previously described. Take a few deep breaths to relax. With your eyes comfortably closed, imagine that a pure, soft, white illumination is slowly permeating your cranium, and you are aware of this soft brightness slowly increasing. Focus on the increasing illumination and don't let your mind wander. Whenever it does and you suddenly realize you've strayed off task, imagine the deep, rich, resonant voice of your best and highest self authoritatively commanding, "In the Name of the Christ, Mind, be still and rest in the Holy White Light."

2. When you finish, record your distractions and any visual hallucinations or vivid mental wanderings you experienced, noting especially if they were visual, auditory, or tactile.

The Third Day's Exercise

Remember, the goal is to discover which types of distractions you are most prone to.

1. Sit in the meditation posture as previously described, making certain that your meditation environment is as completely silent and without sound distraction as possible. Take a few deep breaths, then focus on your ears and the sense of hearing. Listen deeply into your ears until you can hear a thin ringing of sound. It may

sound like the subtle movement of a gentle wind through trees, or like the sixty-cycle hum of an electric speaker, or like a very high-pitched ringing. But it is the subtle, ever-present "background field" for every sound you hear, and it fades or modulates every time a sound intrudes from outside. Be still and focus your attention on hearing that "soundless" sound, and when you hear it listen even more intently with the idea of bringing it closer, louder, and more fully into your consciousness. If your mind wanders, bring it back into line by mentally commanding in a deep, rich, resonant voice "In the Name of the Christ, Mind, be still and listen to the Soundless Sound."

2. When you are finished, record a description of the soundless sound as you heard it as well as any mental wanderings or other distractions you may have experienced, making special note as to whether they were visual, auditory, or tactile.

Analyzing Your Results

At this point, you should have completed your three separate exercises to become familiar with which types of distractions most effectively impede you during meditation—whether they are visual, auditory, or tactile. In other words, are you most distracted by outside sounds, by mental imaginings and wanderings of a mostly visual nature, or by tactile bodily discomforts? At the same time, note whether distractions tend to pull your consciousness into the past (worries, rehashing the day or the week), into the present (outside sounds or motions that are happening at the time of the exercise), or into the future (visual or auditory hallucinations, mental wanderings concerning "what comes next" or plans in process). Note also whether your mind tends to wander into day-dreaming fantasies (active imagination) or night-dreaming, narcoleptic lapses into sleep (unconscious imagination).

From the subjective experience of your own mindscape you may now be able to find answers to the following questions:

- Which of three basic modalities does your mind prefer—visual, auditory, or tactile—or which two does it favor and in what proportions?

- How does your mind try to keep itself attached to mundane, five-sense reality, perpetuate its individual illusions, and resist expanding into the greater awareness that is, for it, a kind of fearsome unconsciousness?

- Which of the three exercises seemed most fruitful to you—that is, which did you enjoy the most, which gave you the feeling that you were good at doing it and could go on for a long time with it?

- Which dimension of time does your mind prefer?

Using Your Results to Design a Strategy to Combat Mental Wandering

Carefully read over your notes about how your mind was distracted. The first exercise had a tactile orientation, the second a visual, and the third an auditory. Look for any patterns, and then knowing the patterns, determine how you might recognize them as they try to manifest during your meditation. Just as the prudent driver learns to recognize his or her own symptoms of drowsiness and pulls off the road before falling asleep at the wheel, the meditator who has studied his or her mental tendencies will be increasingly better able to compensate for wanderings and distractions by "nipping in the bud" whatever begins to arise to pull the mind off task, and thus will achieve increasingly longer periods of focus.

Your results can be used to assist you in maintaining one-pointed focus during Higher Triad Meditation. For example, minds that are most easily distracted by sound are also most open to inspiration or discipline through sound. If you discover that you could most benefit from using auditory techniques to help you control mental wandering, the technique of the wise inner voice, i.e., "In the Name of the Christ, mind be still and rest in the Holy White Light" will probably work best for you. You could also experiment with whispering or humming this phrase.

Minds most easily distracted by tactile sensations are also most open to inspiration or discipline through sensation. If you discover that you could most benefit from using tactile techniques to help you control mental wandering, you might find that swaying back and forth, perhaps a half inch in each direction, will help. Most people will want to combine this with the technique of the wise inner voice, i.e., "In the Name of the Christ, mind be still and rest in the Holy White Light."

Minds most easily distracted by visual imaginings are also most open to inspiration or discipline through use of the imagination. In this case, one can use visualization techniques to control mental wandering. If you discover that you could most benefit from using visualization techniques to help you control mental wandering, try the technique of "mental engraving." This method, discussed by Kaplan in his book *Jewish Meditation*, suggests we imagine engraving or carving words in our imagination. For example, imagine etching on the inner screen of your mind the words "In the Name of the Christ, mind be still and rest in the Holy White Light."

With all techniques for stilling the wandering mind, remember the mind will only be still temporarily. It won't stay still! You will have to tell it over and over again. Every time it wanders off, just bring it back home using whatever method or combination of methods works best for you. When thoughts arise, don't think about them, don't follow them, or cling to them, just notice that you have wandered and gently bring the mind "back home" to the Light.

Finally, if you find that your mental wanderings seem to be more of the active-imagination "day-dreaming" sort, then tip your chin down and lower your eyes to decrease mental stimulation. If, on the other hand, you find yourself having a tendency to get drowsy and fall into fits of vivid unconscious "night-dreaming" while attempting to meditate, try tipping your chin up more and raising your eyes to the horizontal or even a bit higher to stimulate your conscious mental process.

Having made an introductory analysis of your particular mental tendencies, knowing that the channels and modes through which your mind is most easily distracted are probably also the same channels through which your highest and best inspiration comes, you are now ready to take up Higher Triad Meditation.

Beginning the Daily Practice of Higher Triad Meditation

For many individuals, this meditation process will initially feel awkward and cumbersome. Please read through all instructions several times before you begin. Most people will then have to read the instructions to themselves as they complete their first 5-10 times of practice. It is also helpful to learn and practice each phase of this process separately. After a few weeks, you will find you can go through the entire process without reading the instructions. At this point your meditations will begin to feel more natural, authentic, and heart-felt.

Below is an outline of the practice of Higher Triad Meditation. This provides you with the "big picture." After presenting the outline, each phase of the practice will be thoroughly described and explained. Meditation in the Temple of the Holy Grail follows a basic four-fold process:

1. Attunement/Alignment: This involves Prayer and Harmonic Attunement,
2. Communion: This is the actual Higher Triad Meditation,
3. Service: This is the disciplic work of Sending out Blessings, and then
4. Close.

Attunement/Alignment + Communion + Service/Blessing + Close. This four-fold process can also be conceptualized as a even-armed cross. The cross also symbolizes the disciple on the Way.

$$+$$

The vertical arm of the cross represents the aspiring disciple reaching up for Divine Attunement and Alignment. The center of the cross represents the sacred state of consciousness of Communion with the Holy White Light of Christ. The horizontal arm represents the outstretched arms of the disciple engaged in the service of sending out of Blessings.

Another four-fold way of thinking about it would be:

With the Divine, In the Divine, As the Divine, For the Divine

Attunement/Alignment

1. The best time to meditate is first thing in the morning. But anytime is better then no time! If possible, after you wake-up in the morning, go to the bathroom, wash your face, and then meditate for five to ten minutes before eating, talking to anyone or otherwise engaging or stirring up your mind. It is often much harder to meditate fruitfully later in the morning or afternoon because your mind

will no longer be inwardly focussed, as it is for a short while after awakening, but outer-directed to the exterior world. So do it first thing in the morning if at all possible.

2. Go into your meditation room or the special place you have set aside, anoint yourself with rose oil as described in the chapter on *Temple Purity Practices.*

3. Gaze lovingly upon the Face of the Master Jesus hanging over your altar, as described in chapter *The Face of the Master Jesus and the Five Grail Hallows.* Repeat out-loud "I offer this daily sacrificial service for the benefit of all beings" or something similar in meaning.

4. Continue standing in front of your altar, with hands held in prayerful pose at heart level, feel yourself fully present in the Temple of the Holy Spirit (your body). Imagine a silvery cord of light coming out of the top of your head linking you with your Brothers and Sisters in Christ, your Teachers, Gurus, the Masters of Wisdom and Compassion, and especially with your Elder Brother and High Priest the Master Jesus, all existing in The Most High—the One in Whom we live and move and have our Being.

5. Sit with hands held in front and all fingers touching. Visualize the Face of the Master directly before you illuminated in the Golden Radiance from your Heart (as described in chapter nine). From His Heart comes a Crystalline White Radiance that surrounds your head like a halo or crown. Intone the Heart Chakra harmonic as described in the next chapter.

6. Go through the Chakra Attunements (as described in the next chapter) using the finger positions and visualizations described.

End with the Nacham posture (as described in chapter nine) and bow slightly forward toward the Face of the Master.

Communion

1. Rest your hands with palms up on knees or thighs. Make yourself as physically comfortable as possible, but preparing to sit for about five minutes completely still without scratching itches, etc. Close your eyes and inhale slowly through your teeth and tongue with a slight hissing sound very slowly and end in a low, slow exhaled "Hum." Mentally command your mind, "Come Thou Great Light!" or "In the Name of the Christ, Let there be Light." Imagine that a pure, soft, white illumination is slowly permeating your cranium, and you are aware of this soft brightness slowly increasing. Focus on the increasing illumination and don't let your mind wander. Whenever it does and you suddenly realize you've strayed off task, imagine the deep, rich, resonant voice of your best and highest self authoritatively commanding, "In the Name of Christ, Mind, be still and rest in the Holy White Light." Learn to recognize when your mind is drifting and command it to be still. Tell it over and over again. When thoughts arise, don't think about them, don't follow them, or cling to them, just notice that you have wandered and gently bring the mind "back home" to the Light.

2. Keep "looking" straight ahead. "Look" through the single eye from your forehead or bridge of nose. You might get a feeling there is a drawing together of energy and then a distilling and spreading, over and over. You might become aware of a blue field. Around the periphery of the blue field is white light. This is the mechanism of the single eye but you are not seeing anything

through it yet. You're seeing the eye itself or the function of the eye. In the center of that blue field you might be aware of little white spots of light that appear and disappear. That is not what you are looking for. That is all just visual and mental phenomena related to the act of occult seeing. Again, it's from this vantage point you want to mentally command "Come Thou Great Light!" or something similar.

3. Look for gathering gentle clouds of white light distilling in your cranium. For many weeks you may "see" all kinds of things—pinpoints of light, images, etc. But these are all mere mental distractions, or lower astral and mental stages. All you will really do is seek, seek, seek for the Light, then bring yourself back from another wandering and start again. Do not be discouraged! This is the basic stuff you'll work with. It's *a watchfulness, a vigilance.* No images or mental cartoons. It's a seeking—a looking for the Holy White Light. Remember, this Iliaster, this Holy White Light of Christ, is the key to later developments of Initiation, Empowerments, lucid dreaming, astral, and theurgical work. We must develop this consciously for the ability to Bless, heal, and participate in other types of esoteric service. This Holy White Light of Christ is the basic essential stuff which we must be able to evoke in order to do any kind of subtle work. It *must* be a daily practice or it doesn't work.

4. Once the Light begins to manifest, you will lose self-awareness—but that may require many weeks (or months) of regular, daily "seeking" of the Light. Once you finally make contact with the Light, you'll think you've merely wandered again. But then you'll suddenly realize that you were in a state of timeless beauty—without images, without sound, without form, but with Light. The veil will have been rent. At first this breakthrough occurs only for a second or two. Once that

contact is made, the veil has been rent and it's now easier to get to that point. At that point then the meditation should done persistently each day until that state is achieved—if only for a second or two. The whole goal of this type of meditation is to achieve this and then hold yourself in that state. It is an experience of light but a gentle kind of light—the Holy White Light of Christ. You can think of this contact, however brief, as filling up a Sacred and Holy Chalice within your heart—a Cup of Light!

Blessings/Service

1. When you feel that the five-minute meditation is drawing to a close, it is time to send out Blessing. With the "Cup of Light" filled to the brim, even though you may not yet be able to sense it, you can now begin your sacred work of sending out Blessings. The manner in which you do this is highly personal. One suggestion is to offer prayers for those you care about and for world situations that have moved you deeply (as discussed in chapter 5). Another option is to repeat the Great Invocation or participate in the work of the Triangles. One last suggestion is to imagine golden rays of Blessings flowing through you as you repeat "In the Name of the Christ, may the Blessings of the Most High be with all Beings, to the North, to the South, to the East, to the West, above, below, and within. Blessings to all Beings."

Close

1. The manner in which you bring your meditation and service to a close is also highly personal. You will want to do what feels right for you. One method is to make one large sign of the cross with both hands held together as if praying. Begin by holding your

hands over the top of the head and saying "In the Name of the Father." Then bring them down and touch your abdomen and say "and the Son." Then touch them first to your left shoulder and bring them over to your right shoulder as you say "and the Holy Mother Spirit."

2. Then, put your right hand on your left shoulder and cross your left hand over the top to right shoulder. Keeping your hands crossed this way, bow slightly from the waist three times repeating "Amen. Amen. Amen. (pronounced Ah-Main)

3. Give thanks, sit still for a minute or two, and then quietly begin your day.

4. Try to keep your attunement and alignment throughout your daily activities. As Kaplan writes in *Inner Space*, "Perhaps the most important part of meditation is what we do afterwards. It is for this reason that we should strive to internalize the spiritual levels that we attain during meditation and prayer. It is not enough to have an experience; one must be able to hold on to it and make it a part of oneself."

Commitment, Self Discipline, and Perseverance

Meditation is a world service, like prayer, requiring self-discipline, commitment, and perseverance. Remember, even the advanced disciples of Master Jesus found it a hard practice, but it is necessary for the unfoldment of the New World and the New Humanity.

The most important rule about meditation is very simple—JUST DO IT! AND KEEP DOING IT! Alice Bailey in *The Science of Meditation* writes; "The key word in spiritual development is *discipline*. The work is based on the simple premise that energy follows thought and conforms itself to thought. The intention to be of service to mankind is the essential motivation for all true creative meditation. The major safeguard in any course of meditation is simple common sense, and a balanced attitude. With a sense of balance, one realises that progress in consciousness is a long term affair, and that changes do not occur over night. This avoids the disappointment felt by the neophyte when great revelations do not come as promtly as desired."

Just as a musician cannot become a great performer unless he or she invests hours of regular, faithful daily practice on the instrument, so a neophyte cannot develop towards initiation without regular, rhythmic, perseverant spiritual practice.

Recommended Books (available at www.WesternEsotericBooks.com)

Aivanhov, O. (1989). *The book of Divine magic.* California: Provesta, USA.

Bailey, A. *The science of meditation. Pamphlet.* New York: Arcane School.

Kaplan, A. (1991). *Inner Space.* New York: Moznaim Publishing.

Kaplan, A. (1985). *Jewish meditation.* New York: Schoken Books.

Kaplan, A. (1988). *Meditation and the Bible.* Maine: Weiser.

Keizer, L. *Introduction to meditation.* California: Privately Published.

CHAPTER EIGHT
THE TONE OF THE CHRIST

Bishop Keizer in *Harmonic Intoning and Chanting*, writes: "The healing, empowering, evolutionary, and enlightening energies of Higher Reality can be received and utilized only by those who refine and attune their hearts to the subtle frequencies of the Higher Nature. How is this done? As all great Teachings reveal, it is done in a life of service seasoned with interior purification through non-attachment and forgiveness, interior knowledge gained in meditation and vigil, and soul-service carried on through the sendings and architecture of prayer and other rhythmic devotional practice for the common good. Given all this as the esoteric foundation for higher transformation, it is possible to greatly amplify progress and effectiveness through use of sound and music according to the principles outlined here. As we develop interior refinement and sensitivity through self-forgetful service and the inner work of discipleship with the Higher Nature, we build our souls and construct subtle bridges between our gross and subtle bodies. This bridge is called the Rainbow Bridge or in Sanskrit, the antahkarana. We use sound in conjunction with color and form to stimulate, harmonize, synthesize, attune, and waken processes within us that lead to the further building and strengthening of the antahkarana."

Esoteric Science of Vibration and Sound

The correct use of sound is one important method for increasing vibrational frequency and expanding self-conscious awareness. It is important that Templar Initiates develop the skill of mantic and theurgical use of the voice. This is known as harmonic intoning or chanting. It is the key to the Name of God and the sacred AUM, and it is the esoteric science of vibration and sound. Bailey writes: "A mantram, when rightly sounded forth, creates a vacuum in matter, resembling a funnel. This funnel is formed betwixt the one who sounds it forth and the one who is reached by the sound. There is then formed a direct channel of communication."

The voice and the "word" are vital powers of the microcosmic soul dealing especially with energy and vibration. They can be used for various kinds of creative manifestation, such as healing, communication with angelic and elemental beings, working with solar, lunar, and planetary cycles, and—for T∴H∴G∴ Initiates—developing the seven First Order Empowerments of the Temple.

Ancient shamans used harmonic chant with rhythmic drums. Osirian and Isian priests and priestesses used harmonic intoning with the rhythmic seistron. Kabbalistic masters of the Divine Name, Hermetic sages, Hellenistic adepts and magi were secretly instructed in the use of harmonic intoning to make their "rational sacrifice" of praise and Eucharist, or to pronounce the powerful Seven Vowels and the Ephesia Grammata. By the same token, Templar Initiates are taught advanced liturgical use of harmonic chanting for theurgical and other purposes.

Probationers are introduced to the application of harmonic intoning for morning chakra attunements, meditation, and other forms of divine communion. The initial attunement exercises are demonstrated on one of the cassette tapes available as a supplement to this book.

More detailed instruction in the techniques of harmonic intoning are presented in Bishop Keizer's book entitled, *Harmonic Intoning and Chanting: Instruction, Technique, and Esoteric Principles,* which is available through the publications section of the Home Temple web site at http://www.HomeTemple.org. More advanced instruction is given in the Root Chakra and Liturgist Empowerments of the First Order.

Harmonics

What are harmonics? Gardner in *Sounding the Inner Landscape* writes: "For every long tone or single note drone that is sounded or 'struck' whether by voice, an instrument, or in Nature, an entire series of 'unstruck' tones occur simultaneously above that single tone. The struck sound is called the fundamental tone, and the 'unstruck' tones are called harmonics or overtones." For example, if you pluck the 6th string on a guitar, you can hear not only the fundamental tone (E) of that string, but also an entire series of other tones which are multiples of this frequency. For those of you who play guitar, you know that if you place your finger over the 12th fret and slightly dampen the string (without pressing the string all the way down to the fret), you can clearly hear the harmonics.

Attuning through the Crown Chakra

We do not advocate the stimulation of individual chakras. Instead, we recommend attuning them through the Sahashrara Chakra (the Crown Chakra). The crown chakra is the master coordinator for the seven basic chakras we address. We attune our chakras by vocalizing harmonic sounds while simultaneously touching certain fingers together (mudra), and visualizing specific colors and shapes (yantra).

The Generating Tone

The generating tone is simply the key or note you intone (sing). For example, the generating tone we use is normally the note E. The easiest way to learn to duplicate this tone is to buy a tuning key at your local music store. This tuning key looks like a small round harmonica. Each note of the musical scale is listed next to the hole you blow your breath through (again, just like a harmonica). This gives you a clear and pure tone from which to work. After many weeks or months of using your tuning key you should be able to sound the correct note from auditory memory.

The Use of Vowels

By qualifying the generating tone (the single musical note you sing) with vowels that shape the interior of the mouth to produce specific overtones or harmonics, we attune the chakras with first through seventh harmonic overtones. This may sound complicated using the written word but is quite easy to do in practice. Again, it is strongly suggested you undertake more detailed instruction in the techniques of harmonic intoning by acquiring Bishop Keizer's book and tape set entitled, *Harmonic Intoning and Chanting: Instruction, Technique, and Esoteric Principles.*

The Overtone Series

The overtone series is a geometric progression in which the harmonics grow increasingly closer together. The first (Root Chakra) harmonic is an interval of an octave higher; the second (Generative Chakra) a fifth higher than that; the third (Solar Plexus) a fourth (i.e., the second octave); the fourth (Heart) a major third; the fifth (Throat) a minor third; the sixth (Ajna) a minor-minor third; and the seventh (Crown) the interval of a second higher than that—creating the third octave harmonic.

When we learn to hear, produce, and control them, we intone them in conjunction with the following sequence of visualizations and mudras. Mudras are simply certain ways of holding your hands.

Nasalizing our singing or speaking voices will bring out the harmonics and make it easier for you to hear them.

Overview of Daily Practice

As an overview, in your daily practice you will be singing a vowel sound on the note E. While you are intoning this note, you will be simultaneously visualizing specific forms and colors, and touching your fingers together in a specific way (mudras).

Colors

The colors you will use are the spectrum colors of refracted sunlight, and you should study reflected sunlight, rainbows, etc., to learn the hues and subtleties of these colors. It is imperative that they not be dark, but bright and electric. For example;

- The red is rose or blood red;

- Orange is the color of a healthy ripe orange;

- Yellow is the brilliant yellow of the sun;

- Green is the healthy green of well-watered grass in spring—bright and not dark;

- Blue is that of the clear sky at high noon—bright and not dark;

- Purple is like the heliotrope of the setting sun or the purple of a royal robe;

- Violet is bright and electric, like the color of an amethyst.

Shapes

The shapes you will use are best visualized three-dimensionally and as if they were somehow attached to each respective chakra center.

- The Root chakra is attuned visualizing a rose-red Square;

- The Generative Chakra is attuned visualizing an orange Anchor with the sides pointing up;

- The Solar Plexus chakra is attuned visualizing a yellow Circle (a solar disc);

- The Heart chakra is attuned visualizing a green Triangle which points upward;

- The Throat chakra is attuned visualizing an equal-sided blue Cross;

- The Ajna chakra is attuned visualizing a purple Crescent Moon, the horns pointed upward;

- The Crown chakra is attuned visualizing a seven-pointed equiangular violet Star, the top pointed up.

Vowels

Purse the lips and blow as if you were going to whistle, keeping the nose closed while shaping your tongue and mouth as if you were going to create the vowel sound "oh." While still blowing, gradually shape the mouth to "uh," then "ah," then "a," then "eh," then "ih," and finally "ee." As you do this, the shape of your mouth should begin with rounded pursed lips and end up as a full smile with stretched lips as you sound the "ee."

The main idea is that specific vowels, sung on specific tones, using specific shapes of the mouth, will always produce specific harmonics.

Daily Practice (to be done as part of daily Higher Triad Meditation)

Step 1.

Visualize or view the Face of the Master Jesus with both hands extended in prayer-like position in front of you at your heart level (as described in the next chapter). Your right thumb is touching your left thumb, etc., with all fingers touching. Now begin intoning the sound "ah" on the note of E. This is the Heart Harmonic.

Step 2.

Visualize a golden radiance of blessing flowing from your own Monadic Heart Center to surround the Face of the Master in golden light, while his Heart surrounds your Crown with radiant white light.

Step 3.

Begin the rest of the attunement process according to the sequence below. Here you are intoning the various vowel sounds on the E note, touching your fingers together as instructed, while visualizing the associated form and color listed below.

For Root Chakra attunement, begin intoning "OO" on the note of E, while touching just the two thumbs, and visualizing that you are sitting on a rose red square. Do this quickly. It should only take a couple of seconds. You will eventually find you can complete this entire attunement sequence using only one breath.

Continue with your intoning, but shift the shape of your mouth so as to form an "OH" sound. Here, for the Generative Chakra, you are touching only the index fingers while you visualize an orange colored anchor shape sitting in your lower abdominal area.

For the Solar Plexus Chakra, you touch only the middle fingers for the Solar Plexus Chakra, while shaping your mouth to make an "AW" sound. You intone this while visualizing a golden-yellow circle in and around this center.

Now move your attention up to the Heart Chakra and touch just the ring fingers together. Slightly modify the shape of your mouth and/or tongue position to intone the sound "AH." Do this while simultaneously visualizing a Green Triangle at the Heart Center.

Move your attention to your Throat Chakra and touch just the little fingers together. Again, slightly modify the shape of your mouth and/or tongue position to intone the sound "EH." Do this while simultaneously visualizing a Blue Cross at the Throat Chakra.

Move your attention to your Third Eye or Ajna Chakra and touch all five fingers together. Again, slightly modify the shape of your mouth and/or tongue position to intone the sound "IH." Do this while simultaneously visualizing a Purple Crescent Moon at the Third Eye.

Finally, move your attention to your Crown Chakra and touch all five fingers together. Again, slightly modify the shape of your mouth and/or tongue position to intone the sound "EE." Do this while simultaneously visualizing a 7-Pointed Violet Star at your Crown Chakra.

Harmonic Attunement Chart

CHAKRA:	FINGER MUDRA	VOWEL	COLOR/FORM:
Root	Thumbs	OO	Red Square
Generative	Index	OH	Orange Anchor
Solar Plexus	Middles	AW	Yellow Circle

Heart	Rings	AH	Green Triangle
Throat	Littles	EH	Blue Cross
Ajna	All	IH	Purple Crescent
Crown	All	EE	Violet 7-Point Star

Closing

For guidance in harmonic song and chant, one really should learn orally and aurally from a teacher if possible. In the meantime, you will have to practice and experiment. Do so in a resonant private environment, like a bathtub or shower. Eventually you will learn to hear, control, and produce given harmonics at will. The most important harmonic to be able to produce at will is the Fourth Harmonic—the Heart Harmonic. It is your channel to Hierarchy and Divine Communion.

Recommended Books (available at www.WesternEsotericBooks.com)

Bailey, A. (1978). *Letters on occult meditation.* New York: Lucis Publishing Company.

Gardner, K. (1990). *Sounding the inner landscape.* Maine: Caduceus Publications.

Gardner, K. (1998). *Music as medicine: The art and science of healing with sound.* Audio-program. Colorado: Sounds True.

Keizer, L. (1986). *Esoteric principles of song and chant.* California: Privately Published.

Keizer, L. (1999). *Harmonic intoning and chanting: Instruction in vocal technique and esoteric principles of chakra attunement.* California: Home Temple Press.

CHAPTER NINE
THE FACE OF THE MASTER JESUS
AND THE FIVE GRAIL HALLOWS

The Temple of the Holy Grail and its Initiates are guided by many Masters. These Masters, however, work under the instruction and protection of *Mar Yeshua,* the great Master Jesus. The Master Jesus is our Elder Brother in Spirit, the First-Born of a New Humanity. He has opened the Gate of Christhood to humanity by achieving it Himself.

All T∴H∴G∴ Initiates follow the Path of Christhood or the *Imitatio Christi*. This is not simple Christianity or church religion, but a universal mystery school that lies at the esoteric roots of all world religions, whether shamanic or priestly. The Christ is the ancient and future archetype of Perfected Humanity—the collective Being that is the goal of all sentient spiritual evolution in mineral, vegetable, animal, and human kingdoms. Christhood is the more-than-human kingdom of spiritual illumination and liberation from the "world, the flesh, and the devil"—i.e., the illusions of the separative human consciousness, incarnation, and human personal and social evil.

It has been said that the Christ recently assumed the mantle of World Teacher, succeeding the Buddha, who has now advanced into an even broader cosmic work. This is one reason why contemporary humanity must travel the path to Christhood through the insights of Buddhism and Christianity. That is also why the paths of Buddhist Highest Yoga Tantra lead to a form of Christhood producing the Bodhisattva, or perfected Buddha, who (like the Hermetic Saints of the Ogdoad) vows to remain in contact with the lower worlds until all sentient beings have achieved spiritual liberation.

However, a direct contact with the Master Jesus is the most effective path to Christhood. That is because a fully achieved master in any field—whether music, mathematics, or spiritual evolution—emanates from within his or her aura the special energies of attainment that evoke their harmonic response in chelas, disciples, or students. The Master Jesus is like a Sacred Flame that can help us ignite our own interior flames. By drawing near to His presence we "take *darshan*," so to speak, or experience directly the Christ forces and energies within us. Thus, the relics and images of saints have always been considered to be powerful ways of connecting with them and the higher worlds. We have such a relic of the Master Jesus surviving into modern times. It is an image of the historical Face of the Master Jesus.

The Shroud of Turin

The Shroud image is one of five extant historical relics or other physical contacts with the Master Jesus that we designate as Grail Hallows. They help Initiates to take *darshan* of the Master Jesus, who is a living Master. Temple Initiates do a special practice using the Shroud image to strengthen their communion with the Master and the Christ, which will be described later in this chapter.

The medieval Knights Templar used a similar practice. Their most sacred object was what was described at their Inquisition trial as a "head" on a cloth that they "worshipped" and used for magical purposes. It was portrayed by the Inquisitors as a representation of Baphomet, Satan, an heretical survival of Druidism, or some kind of an Anti-Christ. But history shows us that it was the most sacred of all relics, known today as the Shroud of Turin, which has miraculously preserved a full-body and facial image of the Master Jesus.

The image of the Master's Face seen by the Knights Templar, however, was a blurry, indistinct, brownish smudge studied for centuries by church artists to make their images of Christ. It was not the striking image we know today, which is produced by making a photographic negative of the Shroud image.

History of the Shroud

Mary Magdelene picked up the cloth when she found the empty tomb. In the period soon after the crucifixion of Jesus, legend tells us that it was sent to the King of Edessa. He had formally requested a meeting with Jesus, so his disciples sent him the Shroud instead. At Edessa the relic performed many healings and miracles. As a result, Edessa was the first kingdom converted to Christianity.

Later the relic was moved to Constantinople, capital of the emerging Holy Roman Empire. The burial Shroud of Jesus was for many centuries kept in Constantinople folded in such a way as to show only the face. It was called the Mandylion, and the image was faint, fuzzy, and blurred, having apparently been somehow "fixed" onto the linen burial cloth by radiant energy of the so-called Resurrection event. Many centuries later, after a sack of Constantinople by Christian knights during a Crusade, the Mandylion disappeared. It became the property of the Knights Templar. We know this because this is the point in history where all mention of the Mandyion ends, the "head" worshipped by the Templars appears, and the history of the Shroud as a Templar relic begins—in the possession of a Templar family after the destruction of the Order.

In AD 1356 in France, Geoffroy de Charny deposited a long linen sheet in the church he founded. His uncle, after whom he was named, had been a high officer of the Knights Templar before their martyrdom some forty-five years earlier. On this linen sheet it was possible to see what was considered to be the imprint of the face and body of Jesus after crucifixion.

It is recorded that the ruling family of Turin, Italy, bought the Shroud for a huge sum from the widow of de Charny. Apparently he had hidden and protected it after the martyrdom of Grand Master Jacques DeMolay and the attempt by the Pope and Philip the Fair of France to destroy the Order. History records debates from this era about the authenticity of the Shroud of Turin.

From this date forward the Shroud's history is well documented and we know that it arrived in Turin in 1578. Ceded by the last descendent of the Templar de Charny line to the Savoy family in 1453, the Shroud was eventually placed in the Guarini Chapel in 1694. There it remained for some three hundred years as Savoy family property until 1983, when it was willed to the Holy See by Umberto II.

First Photographs of the Shroud of Turin

In 1898 the Shroud was allowed to be photographed for the very first time. The photographs taken that day changed forever the way people viewed the Shroud. When the photographer developed his negative, he was astounded to see the image of the face of Jesus that we now associate with the Shroud. As an image on the cloth it was just a blur. But as a *photographic negative image*, it was visible in graphic detail. Why? Because the image on the Shroud is, itself, like a photographic negative image. When a negative of the image was made, the actual positive image could appear to human eyes. For the first time, the face of the Master Jesus could be seen by the world. Now, little over a century after the photograph was taken, the Shroud has become the most studied religious artifact in human history.

Many relics of saints are medieval fakes. There had been a thriving business in fraudulent finger bones and skulls for the reliquaries of medieval churches, and until recently many scholars had assumed the Shroud was a medieval forgery. Today, however, nearly all scholars and scientists who have studied the relic conclude that it is the authentic burial shroud of the Master Jesus. Complete results of Shroud research are too lengthy to fully describe here, but a summary of some of the more important findings are listed below. Additionally, two Internet web sites are listed at the end of this chapter which provide exhaustive information, resources, and suggestions for further research.

Shroud Research Findings on the Linen Cloth

- The cloth linen is made from materials native to Palestine in the ancient weave native to the period of Jesus.

Shroud Research Findings on Blood Stains and Wound Patterns

- The blood stains match biblical accounts given of the torture and crucifixion, i.e., crown of thorns, spear wound in the side, scourging on the back, etc.

- Blood stains are visible from nail wounds to the *wrists* (not hands) which medical research has shown would be necessary to support the weight of a human body. This contradicts what was assumed in all medieval iconography—that Jesus was nailed through the hands.

- Blood patterns and shape of wounds on the back of the body image *exactly match* patterns which would be made by the archeologically recovered Roman first century tri-tipped Roman whip (an instrument of torture).

- Blood and water from the heart cavity whose drip paths show the exact positions the agonized body turned on the cross over several hours, and much more. Also, his heart and lungs were pierced by a Roman spear, releasing both blood and water (the result of death by crucifixion, which is a form of suffocation that causes water to collect in the heart cavity).

- Wound near the side of torso near fifth rib matches Roman lance.

- The blood tested on the weave of cloth was found to be human blood, type AB.

- John 20: 6-7 states there was a second cloth, possibly a face cloth. This relic exists today, is well documented, and is kept at the Cathedral of Saint John in Oviedo, Spain. It can be dated back to at least A.D. 614 in Jerusalem. Bloodstain patterns are similar to those on Shroud. Blood type of the face cloth is type AB—same as on Shroud.

Shroud Research Findings on the Image of a Human Body

- The image was fixed onto the inside of the cloth only by some little-understood radiant process (not by painting or any other known process).

- The image on the Shroud is holographic, not flat. That is, it was made by radiant energy from a three-dimensional source, rather than painted onto the linen.

- The image is like an x-ray in that it reveals internal structures of the body.

- The blood stains present soaked through the linen cloth and were plainly visible on the back side of cloth, but the image of the human body was not visible on the back side proving the image could not be a painting as painting would have soaked through like the blood.

- The image of the body clearly shows that the thumbs are folded in as they would be from a major injury to the area of nerves around the wrist.

- The stains which make up the image of the body are incredibly complex, i.e., one fiber is discolored while another adjacent fiber is not, the stains are often only the thickness of 1/10 of human hair.

- The Shroud was tested with special Ultra-Violet instruments and it was determined the body image was not made by scorching.

- A VP8 Image Analyzer used by NASA to interpret images from space was used to discriminate two-dimensional images from three. The photo of the Shroud is from a three-dimensional image. This established that the image was formed while draped over a three-dimensional object. By means of a complex series of tests—involving spectroscopy in reflected light, x-ray fluorescence and ultraviolet rays, thermography, radiography, etc.—they confirmed the absolute absence of pigments and dyes on the Shroud.

- All of the evidence shows that the Master's body was far more violently abused than medieval paintings show, and yet his face is completely serene and majestic. This would not have been possible except for a true master.

Shroud Research Findings on Flowers and Pollen Samples

- There are several images of flowers on the Shroud. Research has determined the type of flowers present bloom in March or April, the time the crucifixion is said to have taken place.

- One of the identified plants on the Shroud is known to exist only in Jerusalem.

- Botanical leaf and flower shadows from the mysterious radiant energy that made all of the shroud imprints reveal funery flowers native only to Jerusalem that were placed on the body.

- Pollen samples show a predominance of specimens that grow only in Palestine, and several from only Jerusalem.

- Using state-of-the-art technology which identifies exact pollen types, the type of pollen most present on the Shroud, especially near the head of the image, is from Thistle native to Jerusalem. This was the "Crown of Thorns" that was crushed onto the Master's head.

Other Shroud Research Findings

- Computer analysis compared the face imprinted on the Shroud and some of the principal icons of Jesus' face dating back to the first millennium AD. Work by Giovanni Tamburelli and Nello Balossino in 1989 suggest it is very likely that the face of the man of the Shroud was the prototype of Christian iconography at least since the sixth century.

- Images from coins struck in AD 695 appear nearly identical to the facial image on the Shroud. The inscription on these coins translates as "Jesus Christ, King of Kings."

- Certain caves near Jerusalem contain amounts of a rare type of limestone. On the under side of the Shroud cloth, this rare type of limestone indigenous to area outside of Jerusalem can be found.

- In 1978 Giovanni Tamburelli obtained three-dimensional high definition images from the face of the Shroud highlighting details that would otherwise not be visible. These details included particular traces over the right eyelid. These markings were left by an object identified as being a Roman coin. Coins were used in burial to hold the eyelids shut so that when *rigor mortis* set in, the eyes would not be frozen in the open position. Certain characters of the coin establish a mint date from the first century.

Controversy Over Carbon-Dating Results

In 1988 carbon dating tests concluded the Shroud was no more then 600 years old. Since that time serious doubts have been raised about the accuracy of the carbon-dating results. Most scholars feel that this anomaly—in the face of all the other evidence for antiquity and authenticity—can be explained in one of two ways.

First, is by the radiant energy that created the image in the first place. Was it the Resurrection-event, which occurred in the tomb while the body was wrapped in the Shroud, that radiated or etched the image onto the linen holographically from every part of the body, somehow producing an unknown kind of radiation that contributed to a higher-than-normal C-14 count in the cloth? Or was it some other kind of radiation-producing phenomenon that occurred in the dead body of Jesus? In any case, the radiation that created the image on the cloth could have radically boosted the C-14 percentages in the Shroud linen. Over the centuries, the percentages would have been reduced by half-life to a much higher than normal level, creating the illusion that the Shroud is more than a thousand years younger than it really is.

The other scientific explanation for excess C-14 is that the living mold and bacteria in the linen has kept the C-14 percentages high through its processes of metabolizing carbon from the atmosphere. Normally when a living piece of wood or cloth goes "dead" or is manufactured into something, it stops exchanging gases with the atmosphere and the natural C-14 isotope count slowly decomposes away by half-lives. But when living micro-organisms growing in the linen remain alive, they keep the C-14 percentages significantly high and totally skew radio-carbon dating.

In 1996 fibers from the Shroud were tested and found to have enough of this bio-coating to significantly skew carbon dating results. The linen of the Shroud has been found to be encapsulated in microscopic mold and bacteria that the scientists who did the original radio-carbon dating did not know about and had no effective way to remove.

Physicist Dr. Harry Gove, the inventor of the modern technique of radio-carbon dating stated, "This bacterial contamination is something that the people who did the carbon dating were not aware of," and he recommended a new effort to find ways to remove the bio-coating and do a new radio-carbon dating test.

Currently the Shroud has been sewn to a new backing and placed into a sealed vessel of inert gases, while scientists research ways to remove biological organisms from a sample of the linen that can then be properly radio-carbon dated.

Whatever the case, the face image on the Shroud of Turin was regarded by the Knights Templar to be the Face of the Master, and it is regarded to be so by T∴H∴G∴ Initiates as well. Anyone who gazes upon the Shroud image recognizes intuitively that it is not the face of a crucified criminal, but of a great Master. Those who have the spiritual sensibilities to recognize the

Master's Face are able to derive deep communion in the practice we call the Face of the Master. What is more, the image is not copyrighted. Through modern technology, it is readily and freely available to all who recognize and venerate it.

Other Grail Hallows

The second Grail Hallow is the linen cloth that was placed over the face of Jesus before he was wrapped in the burial Shroud. It has a continuous and well-documented history and is currently housed in a Roman Catholic sanctuary in Italy as previously mentioned. The relic is under the protection of a chivalric order.

The blood on the cloth has been found by scientists to be authentic, and it is of the same rare type AB as the blood found on the Shroud. Moreover, the blood stains on the linen perfectly match the positions of the same stains on the head image of the Shroud. This is because even though his heart was no longer beating, the wounds of Jesus continued to weep after the linen was removed and the shroud placed over his face and body. There is no image on the linen cloth, but its other evidence strongly validates the Shroud of Turin as authentic.

The Spear of Longinus

The third Grail Hallow is known as the Spear of Longinus, but it hasn't the documented authenticity of the Shroud. It is kept on exhibit at the Austrian National Museum and is supposed to be the spearhead used to pierce the heart of Jesus by the Roman soldier Longinus. It has been reconstructed from what is supposed to have been a nail of the True Cross that was plated in gold and tied to a replica of a Roman spear. This relic is reputed to have been held by many of the great Roman generals including

Marcus Aurelius and Constantine, later by Charlemagne, then the leaders of the Teutonic Knights. It was believed that whoever had possession of this relic would triumph in battle and worldly power.

Adolph Hitler, while still an unknown German soldier, sat transfixed before this monument in the Museum and formulated his dreams of world conquest. Later he and his generals constructed a huge retreat center with rooms dedicated to German war heroes to contain this relic, which he had replicated in a detailed copy. When he finally took over Austria in a bloodless coup, his first act was to confiscate the Spear of Longinus and enshrine it in his retreat center.

Years later when Hitler was on the verge of being defeated, he ordered the replica to be hidden in a vault that he knew the Allies would eventually discover in their invasion of Berlin, and the authentic Spear to be hidden elsewhere. However, his curator got the directions wrong in the panic of the invasion and put the authentic Spear into the vault. American soldiers discovered the relic, and eventually it was returned to the Austrian government, where it now remains. This Grail Object is not used by T∴H∴G∴, and its authenticity is not clearly validated.

The Terra Cotta

A fourth Grail Hallow was supposed to have been the terra cotta kiddush cup of the Last Supper held by the aging Templar master in England. You will remember that it was stolen and crushed into the ground. Also stolen were the two subsidiary "grails" or silver chalices that had, by centuries of contact and incubation, assimilated the powers and energies of the original. There is really no way this can be verified. The Chalice of Antioch now on view at the Metropolitan Museum in New York City is supposed to be one of the two subsidiary chalices, and there is a notation on its description that some have claimed it is the true Holy Grail. The other silver chalice is lost.

The Chalice that was made under higher guidance for T∴H∴G∴ is a Grail symbol, but not a Grail Object. It represents the Holy Grail, and it has an intimate connection with the Templar Eggregore that preserved the ancient Graal school. But whether it might ever be stolen or destroyed is immaterial, because the True Grail exists in the Heart of humanity. It is the Path of Christhood and the Initiatic return to Godhead. The Eggregore of the Temple does not empower any objects for strictly magical or selfish uses.

The Hidden Grail Hallow

There is a fifth and hidden Grail Hallow that provides sacred physical contact with the Master. Jesus laid hands upon the heads of his apostles with oil "chrismation" to initiate and ordain them for divine service. They, in turn, laid their hands upon those chosen and trained to succeed them in the work, and they upon the heads of their successors. The sacred lineage of hand-upon-head ordination is a dynamic, potent, and essential Hallow to the Priesthood of T∴H∴G∴, as it was to the Knights Templar, whose Episcopal successions have been passed down to the Temple of the Holy Grail. The historical lineage of the Master's initiation into Apostolic service has been in possession of Catholic, Orthodox, Coptic, and many other churches for two thousand years, but its esoteric properties have rarely been understood or tapped. It is known as the Apostolic Succession.

Apostolic Succession is the lineage of ordination originating with the Master Jesus and his Apostles. It has been carried down through history by the Catholic and Orthodox churches. As opposed to Protestant ministry, which is not a true Priesthood, it can be transmitted only by Bishops who are historical successors of the Apostles. It is also known as the Priesthood of Melchizedek.

This is the Priesthood that was privately received and carried through history by the highest officials of the Knights Templar, who were also

Bishops. This lineage has been restored in the Temple of the Holy Grail. It is discussed in the next chapter.

It provides a subtle physical line of connection with the Master Jesus— from his hands to our heads in sacred ordination. It is also the authority that licenses each Templar as a Subdeacon to handle and use pre-consecrated elements in order to operate the seven First Order Empowerments.

Initiates may choose to undertake training for Apostolic Ordination from the Home Temple under the personal supervision and instruction of the Grailmaster and Grail Mother. Details are given at the following web site: *http://hometemple.org*

FACE OF THE MASTER
INITIAL PRACTICES

Several times daily observe the image of the Master's Face from the Shroud of Turin. Locate a photograph or use the one presented in this chapter.

Get to know each of the details of the Master's Face. It might help to draw the image or work with it on a computer. In any case, begin the process of memorizing the image. Meditate upon the Face of the Master with your eyes open, viewing the image. Then close your eyes and try to reconstruct the image. When you can do this fairly well, try the following exercises:

- In your morning meditation, lovingly gaze upon the Shroud image, then close your eyes. Evoke the White Light. When this is stabilized, visualize your Monadic Heart Center as a radiant field of golden energy extending in a sphere about two feet in all directions. When this has been made stable in your mind, visualize the Face of the Master about fourteen inches in front of you contained within the golden radiance of your Heart. Visualize the Face as being about the size of a silver dollar. Be aware that you are in the Master's presence and hold that consciousness in meditation without wandering or losing focus. When you are done, place your right palm upon your left shoulder and cross your left hand over, with left palm upon the right shoulder. This is called the *nacham* position or mudra, which dynamizes submission to the higher worlds. Bow slightly and give thanks before leaving the conscious presence of the Master.
- Do the same kind of meditation on the exact time of a full moon. Start about five to ten minutes before the exact time of the full moon and meditate until about five minutes after the exact time. Listen, remain totally alert, and keep focused upon the Master's Face. Do *nacham* and give thanks.

These exercises will give you a basis for successfully completing the Heart of the Master Empowerment, which brings you into chelaship or other closer circles within the ashram of the Master Jesus.

References

Shroud of Turin *http://www.shroud.com/menu.htm*
La Sindone http://sindone.torino.chiesacattolica.it/en/welcome.htm

CHAPTER TEN
THE PRACTICE OF
CHIVALRIC SERVICE

"How do we learn to serve? By serving. How do we learn to give? By giving. What is the reward of service? Greater and expanded service."
Mother Jennie (+GM+'s Teacher)

This chapter emphasizes the importance of external as well as internal service in the work of the Temple. It also introduces the reader to other spiritually-focused, service-oriented groups and describes select service opportunities for personal and planetary transformation.

What is Service?

One way to define service is to think of it as making a contribution to the welfare of others. The urge to serve might be experienced as a heart-felt, soul-inspired response to some need we become aware of. This can be the need or situation of an animal, another person, group, community, state, nation, or our planet. We see or hear about a need and feel an urge or inner prompting to take action. It's been said a sense of responsibility is the first major expression of soul contact; the second, an urge to serve (give/share).

Saraydarian, in his book, *The Ageless Wisdom*, tells us, "The whole aim of the student of the Ageless Wisdom must be: How can I make myself ready to be useful in meeting the needs of humanity in higher and higher fields of responsibility?"

Looking at service from another angle, it can be seen as an exchange of force and energy. From this view, what we call "giving" is the streaming out of forces and energies received from higher non-physical levels. To use an analogy, we could say the body is to soul, as wire is to electricity and just like electricity, for flow to occur it needs a third point outside itself. The point is this: if energy flows down from higher levels to the physical world, (like electricity flowing through a wire), and if the body is where these potential energies are stored (like an electrical capacitor), then in order to flow (or discharge) they must be grounded and connected to another point outside oneself. Without giving (providing an outlet), blockage can occur. Using this example we can voluntarily, consciously, and purposefully serve as a conduit for love to flow into the world. The following formula suggests how this can be done:

Invoke (ask for blessing) → Commune (receive blessing)→
Serve (distribute blessing)→ Evoke (return blessing)

This is a basic formula used to develop the Practices of the Blessing Way taught in the Temple, and it is the ancient meaning of the Biblical Greek and Hebrew concept of "blessing," meaning "to return blessing to God," and encompassed in the more ancient Egyptian High Priestly Nile blessings. That is what is meant by "blessing God," as in the Jewish *kiddush* prayer, "Blessed art Thou…" or "We bless Thee…" Ultimately, all invocation becomes evocation, because our Divine Being is awakened, activated, and exercised from within our own Hearts, and we and all connected with us are therefore *transformed* in and by the process of service. By invoking the Higher Nature, we evoke its essential qualities within our own interiors.

"Put aside all prejudices and, summoning thy spiritual forces, aid mankind. Not for revelations, but for service, did I summon thee."

—*Master Morya*

Esoteric Sharing

Sharing is the ability to make energy circulate. Any flow that is hindered or blocked creates short circuits, congestion, and destruction. Sharing is a good way to get rid of all your blocking, selfish, and greedy elements. If you don't, these elements crystallize in your nature and pave the way for your future failures. They are dissolved by the fire of sharing. For example, think of abundance as an energy flow. Think of selfishness and greed as a greasy hair-ball clogging up the pipe and preventing the free-flowing of prosperity.

The Teachings advise you to organize your life in such a way that you always give. Give your wisdom, your guidance, your love, your serenity, your money, your labor, your energy, and Mother Nature will give back to you with high interest. Master Jesus is reported to have said: "Unto those who give, even more will be given to them. Unto those who do not give, the things that they have will be taken from them."

Recognizing Service Opportunities

Many people ask, "What can I do? I'm only one person." They don't realize that service is effective as is effort and motivation, whether or not it is visibly successful in attaining a given end. It is the means, not the end, that is of first importance.

Need is always present around us; for example, in our relationships with family, friends, and associates. Here, working on an individual basis, we have opportunities to practice patience, compassion, right-thought, right-speech, right-action, and right-employment.

In the privacy of our homes each of us can serve via personal purity practices (as described in the next chapter), meditating, intercessory prayer, blessing, helping, writing, teaching, mentoring, counseling, healing, donating, creating inspiring works of joy and beauty, and many other ways. Each of us can make a commitment to do a deeper study of one of the many problems of humanity and then do something to help resolve it. We can pay attention to what is going on in the world and take notice of examples of goodwill in action. We can meditate and ponder over concepts like unity, synthesis, truth, goodness, beauty, joy, compassion, peace, and thus help strengthen the collective thought-form of these vital energies and then apply our learning's in daily life.

We can help send forth light into the world via daily participation in the network of Triangles. We can link mentally with countless others in sending daily prayers for our President, the United Nations, and other world leaders that they will be inspired to do what is best for all humanity—regardless of our personal opinions of them. We can participate in several special meditations that take place on a daily, weekly, monthly, and annual basis. We can also participate in liturgical and other focused group work.

True, the need is overwhelming and we all must work in accordance with our own limitations. We are reminded, on the other hand, that as personalities, we often underestimate our capacities. One of the purposes of this section is to suggest that you personally can make a positive difference and to give you ideas and resources for doing so.

Considering the distribution part of the formula previously described, we can ask ourselves: Who are the people I can help today? How can I help enhance goodwill and right human relationships? How can I help spread love and understanding? Who can I pray for?

If we feel drawn to help children, we might look into volunteering for organizations such as Guardian Ad Litem or the Big Brother/Big Sister program. If we feel drawn to work with seniors in need, we may consider working as an Omsbudsman, for Hospice, or helping out with Meals on Wheels.

Collectively, we can participate in Internet-based forums such as the World Transformation Organization. We can seek out our brothers and sisters in the New Group of World Servers and support/join with them in their endeavors. We can participate in any worthy charitable organization involved in providing basic human needs or protecting human rights such as Unicef, Childreach, the International Red Cross, Amnesty International, the United Nations, www.thehungersite.com, or hundreds of others listed on Internet Web sites such as One World On-Line or at www.EsotericWorldService.org.

> *"You will ask what your service is to be? That will grow out of your meditation. It is not for me to tell you what activity your personality must follow, it is your own soul which must do so."*
>
> —*Master DK*

As the Tibetan Master Dwal Khul states: "I care not where or to who you give, only that you give—little if you have but little of time and money, much if you have much. Work and give, love and think, and aid those groups who are building and not destroying, loving and not attacking, lifting and not tearing down. I ask you to recognize your fellow workers in all groups and to strengthen their hands. I ask you to seal your lips to words of hatred and of criticism, and talk in terms of brotherhood (and sisterhood) and of group relations. If you cannot teach or preach or write, give of your thought and of your money, so that others can. Give of your hours and minutes of leisure, so as to set others free to serve the Plan; give of your money, so that the work of those associated with the New Group of World Servers may go forward with rapidity."

As the great Master Jesus taught: "It is better to give than to receive. It is in giving that the soul prospers...for in the measure that you give will it be measured out to you, for good or for ill; therefore do unto mankind as you would have heaven do unto you…and from him who little has been given, little will be required; but from him unto much has been given, much will be required…to those who use what they have, more will be given; but for those who neglect or abuse it, even what they have will be taken away."

"Faithfulness without works is dead; for faith consists of deeds, and not words…in as much as you have done it unto the least of these my brethren, you have done it unto me."

—*Master Jesus*

The Essence of Chivalry

Ellwood in *The Cross and the Grail* reminds us: "selfless giving is the essence of chivalry, that code of the Medieval Knights who served King Arthur and the grail, and who are our ideal in the romantic and esoteric side of Christianity. As embodiments of chivalry, esoteric Christians are expected to always serve the poor, protect the weak and labor for justice among persons and nations. The faith allows no discrimination or injustice among its members, or in society on the basis of creed, race, gender, sexual orientation, relative wealth or poverty, education or lack thereof. To fulfill this ideal, every Christian should have an ongoing commitment to the important labor of unpaid, volunteer work and should try to be a peacemaker whenever possible. The only means by which an action can finally be judged is whether it enhances and increases love in the world." The same applies to esoteric Jews, Muslims, Hindus, Buddhists, Humanists, and anyone else seeking social and personal divine transformation.

St. John, in his first epistle, states that love for others, for our neighbor, the child, the defenseless, is the only test of sincerity in any claims of love for God. Ellwood goes on to say: "This, then, is the command that Christ gave us, 'He who loves God must love his brother also,' loving the neighbor, binding wounds, feeding the hungry, giving drink to the thirsty, receiving the stranger into our home, clothing the naked, caring for the sick, visiting those in prison, caring for the child. These are imperatives addressed to all of us."

Eliphas Levi, in *The Key of the Mysteries*, states: "The Great Master, in one of his parables, condemns only the idle man who buried his treasure from fear of losing it in the risky operations of that bank we call life. To think nothing, to love nothing, to wish for nothing, to do nothing—that is the real sin. The man who isolates himself from every human love, saying 'I will serve God,' deceives himself. For, said St. John the Apostle, if he loveth not his neighbor whom he hath seen, how shall he love God whom he hath not seen?" He goes on to write: "Nature only recognizes and rewards workers. To do nothing is as fatal as to do evil, but it is more cowardly. The most unpardonable of mortal sins is inertia. The most fatal energy of our souls is idleness. Inertia intoxicates us and sends us to sleep. The true evil. That for which there is no remedy, is inertia. God has often made saints of scoundrels, but He has never done anything with the half-hearted and the cowardly."

In *The Ageless Wisdom*, Saraydarian writes, "A student of the Ageless Wisdom never advances unless he learns how to serve and unless he finds daily opportunities to serve others in joy and without self-interest."

What situation moves you the most to want to act in your home, community, nation, or world? Is there a particular group or sector that you feel drawn to serve? Do you feel a tug on your heart strings when you hear, read about or encounter a certain type of social problem or issue? Follow that tug.

"The man who can keep his fingers fast closed on his purse and pass by another man who he has reason to believe is homeless and hungry; who can refrain from opening that purse while a wounded beggar, or a sick child lies in a hovel or on the street through which he must pass to his own comfortable home, could not by any possibility face the Master at the top of the great Initiation Stair."

—Master Hilarion

Recommended Books (available at www.WesternEsotericBooks.com)

Bailey, A. (1971). *Ponder on this.* New York: Lucis Publishing Company.

Ellwood, R. (1997). *The cross and the grail: Esoteric Christianity for the 21stcentury.* Illinois: Quest Books.

Saraydarian, T. (1990). *Ageless Wisdom.* California: T.S.G. Publishing.

Saraydarian, T. (1977). *Triangles of fire.* California: Aquarian Educational Group.

CHAPTER ELEVEN
ANTAHKARANA BUILDING WITH
FRAGRANCE AND INCENSE

The subtle links—the continuity of consciousness—between the human and the divine were broken ages ago. As humanity began to incarnate, to develop as the microcosmic soul or universal species, and individuate, each human incarnation fell further away from conscious awareness of its divine origin until the extreme nadir of this descent into gross matter had been reached.

Humanity began its return homeward long ago. Ancient mystery religions and medieval initiatic schools taught about the restoration, reintegration, resurrection, or apotheosis of a future perfected human archetype—soul by individual soul. Ideals of Christhood, Buddhahood, and other forms of human perfection are widely known in modern religion.

However, human mental consciousness has polarized in the brain to the point that it has become highly linear, discursive, and objectified. There is a blockage or, as Gautama would say, a "knot" in the flow of subtle consciousness that separates each person from the higher, divine awareness that speaks with a "still, small voice."

One of the major works of contemporary spiritual process is to withdraw from the gross and overpowering voices of the outer physical world and seek the internal worlds, which exist on many levels: biochemical, energetic, emotional, psychological, and noetic, to name a few. Meditation, contemplation, harmonic intoning and attunement, liturgy, mantra, mudra, divination, and other resources must be employed to either elevate the Heart sensibilities into mental consciousness, or to assist us to descend in consciousness into the sensibilities of the Heart.

All of the gross senses have subtle octaves that must be developed by spiritual practice. Physical sight is an externalization of the dormant power of clairvoyance; hearing is an externalization of clairaudience; smell, of general intuitive faculties; taste, of discriminatory intuition; spatial touch, of telemetric powers; and dynamic tactile feeling, such as heat, of the sensibilities of psychic love, compassion, soul-travel, and spiritual merging.

The Rainbow Bridge

Each of these "broken links" exist as subtle spirillae and webbings that can be developed and grown into full continuity of consciousness between ordinary mental consciousness and the multiple octaves of higher selves and ego-states that connect us with spiritual Hierarchy and our divine origins.

The sum total of that organism has been called the Antahkarana, the Rainbow Bridge that connects incarnate perceptions to divine Reality. In addition to the many Temple practices and the daily chakra attunements designed to help restore that Bridge, we do the Antahkarana Building Empowerment one solar cycle, or one full year, after Initiation—on the following year's Wesak Moon.

However, the sounds, odors, and other disharmonious energies of a human society that remains grossly alienated from divine consciousness and sentiments have a destructive effect on those who strive to transcend. We are like snowballs in hell. Without special protections and techniques, we will soon dissolve and flow into the lower levels. The following chapter on Imperil discusses the special protections Templars can use against these energies, as well as the techniques for developing not only immunities, but the ability to transform and thrive upon the distillations of these formerly negative energies.

Esoteric Use of Fragrance

One of the major protective means of reinforcing continuity of divine communion is by esoteric use of flower fragrances and tree incenses. The human olfactory or sense of smell interacts with a major portion of the brain, but has become increasingly dormant as a feature of unconscious processes. For this reason, fragrance can be used to access the unconscious mind. It can activate both subconscious memories, fears, and joys, or subtle links to the superconscious mind. In Temple practices, however, we use essential oils and fragrances to both antidote negative energies that try to invade through the auric egg, and to sweeten our auras for continuity of consciousness with our higher nature.

Mineral, plant, and animal essences (Paracelsus would refer to the Mercury, Sulfur, and Salt of plants) have not just physical bodies and aspects, but etheric, astral, and—in the case of minerals—mental plane characteristics. Their entities or collective souls are rooted in these more subtle worlds. Thus, they can affect and heal human psychic elements when inhaled or eaten. That is why alchemical, spagyric, and homeopathic remedies work for people who have more developed psychic sensitivities.

Temple Practice—Daily Application of Rose Oil

Purchase a bottle of the best Rose essential oil you can find (should be about $10 to $20 for a dram or a small bottle). Bless or consecrate it by holding it to your Monadic Heart Center (on a straight line midway between Adam's Apple and Solar Plexus—hereafter called the "Heart"), visualizing golden-white radiance coming from your Heart and surrounding the bottle, which you hold in your left hand, with your right hand cupped over it. Intone an AUM Blessing as you make the visualization with focused Blessing intention. Do this whenever you get a new bottle of

Rose oil. Do this Blessing with any medicine, pills, or special food or drink you intake, including the Eucharistic Host. In public you must do this silently.

Apply a small amount of the consecrated Rose oil to the following parts of your anatomy every morning before dressing, using an equal-sided cross motion from top down, then your left to your right on each location:

- Crown
- Ajna (between the eyebrows)
- Nape of Neck; Throat (Adam's Apple)
- Monadic Heart Center
- Solar Plexus
- Either in the folded crease between upper and lower arm where blood is drawn, or on the underside of the wrist (these are referred to as the "Pulses" in Templar terminology)
- And either in the folded crease between upper and lower legs, or on the soles of the feet

These constitute ten positions in eight locations. When you have been Initiated, add a small amount of Amber oil to your Rose and continue the practice.

If you are meeting with people whose respect and cooperation you need, or doing some kind of creative presentation or performance later in the day or evening, reapply oil to the Throat and Heart soon beforehand. Don't overdo and make the fragrance overpowering. It should remain subtle—preferably just below the threshold of consciousness. You will find that the subliminal effect will vastly increase your probability of making a good impression, gaining cooperation, or bringing off an inspired presentation or performance.

The following pages reproduce the Fragrance and Incense Manual used in the Home Temple Priesthood, and are included here for your information.

Esoteric and Liturigal Use of Fragrance

NARCISSUS

Blooms mid-winter to spring in California, six white lotus-like petals, three golden anthers on green stem, grow from bulbs. Extremely fragrant as flowers. Associated with:

- the color Gold
- Beauty
- Regeneration
- Solitude and
- relates to the Lotus power of Transformation

Use in practice:

- Use with Rose for high spiritual communion, add Amber for high manifestational work and liturgies
- Dissolves Imperil
- Use on New Moon for beginning and seeding projects
- Use in labor room for birth, healing of children, bonding in adoption of children, healing of women from afflictions of female organs
- Guidance from fairy world may be invoked with name, "Narcissus"

WHITE LOTUS

Associated with:

- color heliotrope or violet
- power of Spiritual Transformation

Use in Practice:

- Special liturgical olfactory and visual symbol, color heliotrope or violet. Opens specific chakra when placed on skin location for specific work, then WASH OFF TO AVOID IMBALANCE

Example: Use on Throat for powerful manifestational work with AUM

- Use in liturgies of transformation, alchemical work, initiatic liturgies
- Use with psychological and mental healing—drug addiction, etc.—as a subtle catalyst to facilitate positive transformation

GARDENIA AND JASMINE

Jasmine is lower octave, Gardenia higher octave of power called Purity and Beauty. Must be pure of heart and mind (no crudity or half-hearted habituality) to work with this essence. Associated with:

- Mother of the World, Virgin Mother, Sacred Family
- Universal Love and Compassion
- the color Rich Blue-Purple
- Archangelic world and its divine perfection

Use in Practice:

- For all Bodhisattva practices, visualize self with a thousand hands, each with a sensitive, conscious eye in the palm, directing Compassion in rich blue-purple rays unto all need
- Use for all anonymous and unseen service to link with the Ray of the Christ and the Bodhisattva
- Use for works of Love for love's sake only
- Use on Throat, Ajna, and Palms, and Pulses
- Use also as oneiropompos or high spiritual dream-bringer on Crown and Ajna (Gardenia only)
- Use for healing done from a distance and invisibly. Use also when working with plants and children to facilitate flow of effective rays
- Facilitates memory and healing or skill with fingers, toes, extremities (Jasmine). Gardenia can be used in Radiance work and healing
- Facilitates contact with Archangelic kingdom. Gardenia can bring assistance from specific Archangels of Briah by name (Michael,

Raphael, etc.). Jasmine can aid invocation of Archangelic rulers working in Yetzirah

ROSE

While symbolism of various colors and kinds of rose varies, the essential fragrance has basic powers of Spiritual Beauty, Communion, and Presence. It dissolves imperil-forming irritations and creates a spiritual radiance in the aura of a person or place.

Use in Practice:

- Apply daily before morning meditation to Crown, Ajna, Throat, Heart, Solar Plexus, Nape of Neck, Pulses, and Soles of Feet
- Use as incense for all spiritual gatherings and communions as well as private meditation
- Inhale from time to time during the day but not before bedtime
- Rose oil is like element Copper and power of Venus—it can be a medium to unite the powers of all other fragrances for specific works and purposes
- Works with Amber for healings, consecrations; but not exorcisms
- Use on hands when doing any healing, ordination, or other radiation of divine power through hands, then wash with water up to elbows after finish

AMBER

Potentiates the flow and accumulation of Psychic Energy and Prana. Puts energies of aura into flux. Good uses for higher communions, attracting of higher spiritual powers for lecturing and doing all kinds of Throat Chakra work; but do not use when contacting with dark forces or negative psychic energies. Use on Solar Plexus and Nape of Neck (the two openings for obsessive consciousness) ONLY for work with powers of Light.

Use in Practice:

- Mix with Rose for ordinations, consecrations, Temple incense
- Apply to Ajna, Throat, Heart for manifestational and radiance work (higher adepts apply also to Solar Plexus and Pulses, and even to all points for certain works). Other uses not disclosed at this time
- Use on hands mixed with Rose when channeling pranic healing (broken bones, weakened system, etc.—but not for viral and germ-caused contagious disease. Otherwise enlivens micro-organisms

EUCALYPTUS/SANDALWOOD/PINE AND DEODAR
These can all be used for exorcistic and general Astral clearing.

PEPPERMINT/ROSEMARY/LAVENDER
These can be used with Amber to facilitate psychic energy. Rosemary and Lavender are used together for operations requiring balance of masculine and feminine, or right and left channel, forces, such as Equinox.

FREESIA
Can be used for Angelic levels of Gardenia and Jasmine work and to invoke Angels of Yetzirah by name.

OLIVE
Can be mixed with many other fragrances moderated by Rose for Ordination and Consecration oils. Used to transmit Psychic Energy and Pranic Healing, Ordination, by Hands.

WORMWOOD
Dissolves Imperil.

CHAPTER TWELVE
POLISHING THE CHALICE: IMPERIL AND ESOTERIC PURITY PRACTICES

What is imperil? How is it created? Why should the contemporary disciple be concerned about imperil? How can the negative effects of imperil be reduced or eliminated? Addressing these questions and providing techniques you can immediately apply to help reduce the negative effects of exposure to imperil-producing irritants is the main focus of this chapter. These techniques include use of certain fragrances, oils, resins, tones, colors, cleansing breath, and juice.

Concerns About Imperil for the Contemporary Disciple

Disciples routinely engage in various purity practices to help eliminate obstacles to spiritual sensitivity. Disciples have historically experienced a need to do the work of spiritual purification alone and away from the often coarse vibrations of civilization. For example, in the past, it was common for a disciple to seek this solitude on a mountain or in an isolated cave.

Today's disciple is likely to live in a city. For today's disciple the way of living can also be a way of serving—being in life, staying in life, like the ideal of the Buddhist Bodhisattva who returning to life, incarnation after incarnation, works for the purification of the planet and the liberation of all sentient beings.

In this new situation where we find ourselves in, there are new kinds of dangers and environments that have to be lived in and dealt with. The basic category this danger comes under is called "Irritation." Those that become psychically sensitive can become easily irritated. But irritation in this sense is more than just a mental and emotional state. Irritation is an actual astral and etheric state.

Alice Bailey (1982) writes: "Irritation is exceedingly prevalent these days of nervous tension and it most definitely imperils progress and retards the steps of the disciple on the Way. Irritation definitely generates a poison which locates itself in the region of the stomach and of the solar plexus. Irritation is a disease, if I might use that word, of the solar plexus center and it is definitely contagious to an almost alarming extent. So, my brothers, watch yourselves with care and remember that just so far as you can live in the head and in the heart, you will end the disease of imperil and aid in the transference of the forces of the solar plexus in to the heart center."

The product of irritation in the astral level is a crystallization, a precipitate, a sediment that deposits itself in the channels known as "nadis," the nerve channels, a kind of black, fiery substance known as "Imperil." It settles in these chakra networks and burns the fine complex structures of the astral and etheric bodies and results in an ever-increasing contractedness of personality and of consciousness. It can then degrade our higher, psychic, and subtle sensibilities making us become more gross and insensitive to divine guidance and spiritual impulses.

Imperil is highly contagious and can be spread by touch, sound, food, etc. Imperil is a poison that people encounter more and more as they become sensitive, more tuned, and more developed on the Path. Irritation and the imperil it forms is one of the first challenges the disciple must deal with.

Subtle Anatomy and the Need for Esoteric Purity

Each human soul is an extension of a ray or emanation of Godhead known as a divine Monad. These Monads continually come into manifestation. Some human souls, (complex holons of many ancient psychic elements that have been brought into harmonic unity over aeons of incarnation), are "old souls," and some are relatively young.

Each "older human soul" stands upon its own individual step of the Anodos or Path of Return to God. Younger and less individuated souls stand in groups upon different steps.

The human soul is qualified into manifestation on all planes of existence by bodies. The incarnate human soul exists in three kinds of bodies expressed through many levels of density. These correlate to the Lower Triad, Chalice, and Higher Triad groupings of the seven chakras. The Lower Triad consists of the Root, Generative, and Solar Plexus. The Chalice consists of the Solar Plexus, Heart, and Throat. The Higher Triad consists of the Heart, Throat, and Head (includes Ajna and Crown).

The Lower Triad relates especially to the gross physical body and the electromagnetic fluids or ethers that constitute the four etheric bodies. They permeate and extend outward from the physical body as the Earth's watery, gaseous, and electromagnetic atmospheres interface with the rare substances and energies of space. Thus, the incarnate physical human body is not a separate or discreet entity unto itself, but is merely the most gross, densified, and compact part of the psychic organism.

The etheric bodies expand outward from the physical body in an egg-shaped aura. This aura may extend anywhere from a foot to *ten or twenty feet* from the apparent limit of the material body, depending upon many factors, one of which may be spiritual development. It is through these media that what we think of as "possession" of human vehicles operates, and through the Solar Plexus or Generative chakras in particular.

These, in turn, interface with extremely expanded levels of astral and mental bodies that permeate those of all other human beings and, in adepts, expand toward infinity. They relate especially to the Chalice, which stores all experience in the *akasha* and carries it as non-discursive karmas, traits, and talents from incarnation to incarnation of the growing soul. It is through the Solar Plexus and Throat—especially the area around the nape of the neck—that obsessive astral and mental forces gain entrance. They attach like parasites, drawing upon vital etheric energies to delay their inevitable decay back into elemental psychic particles that, after purification, can once again begin the aeons of evolution and psychic marriages required to attain the status of a human soul.

It is through aspects of the Chalice that most psychic "channelings" are done. Most of these channelings are from astral entities, not masters or high spiritual beings. However, in rare cases an incarnate master like Koot Hoomi might, with permission and special training, speak through a psychically talented chela like Helena Blavatsky.

Beyond these are Buddhic and Atmic bodies that encompass the entire Macrocosm. It is they who relate especially to the Higher Triad. Advanced spiritual initiates can receive impressions and lessons from discarnate spiritual masters and angelic beings dwelling in these planes of Reality through the process of overshadowing or "overlighting." These higher triad psychics work through intuitive faculties to transmit spiritual teaching and guidance.

The etheric aura can be visualized for practical purposes to extend the same distance from our bodies that we can measure by extending both arms. It can be developed by using the invoked light of the First Iliaster to create protective aquastors. These protective aquastors eventually render the aura impenetrable to all but the most potent invasive forces and energies. This is done in the First Empowerment after Initiation in the Temple of the Holy Grail.

Part of this protection, however, lies in dealing intelligently with negative forces that can invade, pollute, and permeate the auric egg. Part of their power is because they are not seen, known, or recognized. Dark forces operate most effectively on a subliminal level. Knowing how these forces are generated and the conditions that concentrate them is vital for Initiates, because they are attracted to enhanced spiritual light like moths to a flame.

New Initiates of the Temple deal first and immediately with the Empowerment Over Dark Forces, as by virtue of their Initiation they become extremely vulnerable to psychic attack. However, they exist under the protection of the Eggregore of the Temple which, in combination with the First Empowerment and the Purity Practices to be outlined below, provide excellent stability.

A Closer Look at Imperil

What is imperil? Roerich (1981) writes: "Imperil is the designation given by the Great Teachers to the poison of irritability." The word "imperil" was first made public in the Agni Yoga books by Helena Roerich. The Tibetan Master DK mentions imperil in the books by Alice Bailey and Torkom Saraydarian greatly expands the practical methods for working on imperil in his books, especially *The Psyche and Psychism*, chapter 27. Irritation in its many forms are the cause of imperil. Bailey (1971) writes, "more lives are ruined by irritation than can be counted."

Irritation is a fire that appears in the aura and spreads. If irritation is not metabolized properly, it can form into a by-product of black, fiery-crystals. These black, fiery-crystals are imperil. Imperil is a crystallized astral/etheric sediment that lodges in the nadis (or nerve channels) as a result of irritation, anger, fear, or depression.

Imperil invades and pollutes our auric energies when it is taken inside by breathing, eating, or through the senses (sight, sound, etc.) or the mind (negative ideas and suggestions). It can then degrade our higher, psychic, and subtle sensibilities making us become more gross and insensitive to divine guidance and spiritual impulses. It collects in population centers, where it manifests as aeroperil permeating the atmosphere. Initiates who live or must work in large cities must take special care to do Purity Practices and use rose oil daily.

Technological Threats to the Etheric Web

There are forces other than imperil that keep spiritual initiates from developing, such as the multitudes of radio waves that permeate our environment. They come from radio, television, short wave, microwave, and other kinds of transmissions that have been increasingly broadcast everywhere since the twentieth century.

These forces can knock holes into the growing etheric spirillae of the Antahkarana, much as nuclear radiation bombards living cells with subatomic "bullets." If not too much is absorbed, the cells might be able to replace what has been destroyed and heal. But if too high a dosage has been absorbed, the cells die. It is the same with our etheric webs. They are constantly shot through with electromagnetic bullets that undo their progress. The same effect occurs with X-rays.

Fortunately, there is a simple remedy for this twenty-first century malady. It is pomegranate juice. It has several esoteric properties, one of which is that it stimulates healing and rebuilding of etheric webbing. It is also used for the Sacramental Chalice in Empowerments.

Common Causes of Imperil

Imperil is generated by sentient psychic beings when they experience hatred, fear, worry, discomfort, and disease. It is generated more powerfully by sentient beings with complex souls than those with simpler souls.

That is why the flesh of slaughtered mammals contains far more concentrated Imperil than that of fish or fowl.

By eating red meat, we intake large doses of imperil into our auric egg, and that is the reason the ancients espoused vegetarian diets for spiritual work. However, advanced spiritual practitioners (like the Vajrayana tantric masters) learned to not only make themselves immune to Imperil consumed in red meat, but to transform it and even thrive on it.

Contrary to the claims of some, and in contrast to John the Baptist, the Master Jesus did not appear to use a special diet. He ate meat and drank wine. But he remained internally pure and even warned his disciples that true impurity came not from the outside, but from acting upon the wrong impulses of the heart—from within.

For this reason, *it is possible to purify all pollutions through the Divine Energies of the Heart.* However, while the T∴H∴G∴ Empowerments work to develop this kind of interior spiritual power within you, it will be necessary to avoid overdosing yourself with imperil and to undertake special Purity Practices to help your psycho-spiritual faculties to grow to this point.

But the most potent generators of imperil are human beings with the effects of civilization—their institutions and societies. People are constantly creating imperil and qualifying it into the atmosphere with breath and into the ground through the soles of their feet as they walk upon the Earth.

Humanity has alienated itself from nature and the Mother Earth by its abuse of the mineral, vegetable, and animal kingdoms—and most potently by its abuse of the human kingdom. The blood of a human victim spilled upon the Earth creates an *extreme* pollution, even a curse. Perhaps this is one reason why the Earth is a place of earthquakes, extreme weather, dangerous wild animals, and poisonous plants.

As humanity reconciles itself with Mother Earth and all the sentient beings it has abused, and as humanity begins to manifest the Divine Nature hidden within its Heart, the Earth will become a Paradise. That is what the adept Paul said, "The Cosmos awaits with eager longing the appearance of the New Humanity…because the Cosmos Itself will be liberated from bondage to decay, and will Itself obtain the glorious liberation of the New Humanity." (Romans 8.19...20)

The following is a list of the major causes of imperil.

- Agitation in the astral body, i.e., stress, anger, fear, depression
- Hatred, prejudice, revenge, feelings of resentment
- Being around others who are critical or gossiping. The old saying of the Masters is, "When there's pepper in the air everyone sneezes!" When there is imperil in the air everyone gets it!
- Ingratitude/intolerance
- Impatience (major source)
- Worry, lying
- Violent or sexually graphic movies
- Red meat
- Abuse of drugs
- Noise pollution, loud music
- Places of war, crime, suffering, pains, sorrow, etc., are imperil pits
- Public phones
- Library books
- Handshakes, hugging, kissing, intercourse
- Imperil is highly contagious and can be spread by touch, sound, food, etc.

Temple Purity Practices

1. Daily harmonic chakra attunement (as explained in chapter 8).

2. Daily use of rose oil (as previously described in chapter 12).

3. Purchase pure pomegranate juice from a health food store and drink a few teaspoons at least once a week. You can mix it in other juices if you find the taste too strong, but eventually you will find that you develop a

taste for pomegranate juice. When that happens, you will know that the accumulation of imperil in your auric egg is starting to reverse.

4. Use a Sterilizing Breath. When you use a public telephone or touch other things that are probably permeated with imperil, use the Sterilizing Breath on the surface. Always use Sterilizing Breath after negative or positive contact (cleansing from obsession, imperil, healing, projecting of Blessing, etc.). With conscious intent and focused will, use COLD, DRY Sterilizing Breath. Blow with quick, explosive motion through pursed lips with conscious separation from object to be cleared (like you are blowing dust off something).

5. Use Temple Soap. Use a very small amount of wormwood oil to make Temple Soap along with equal parts of eucalyptus, peppermint, and lavender. The easiest way is to use Dr. Bronner's castile soaps and mix them, adding about ¼ teaspoon of wormwood oil to two pints of mixture. You can shower in the special soap before doing the auric cleansing intoning from time to time—perhaps once every few months—in addition to using the procedure for Initiation and Empowerments later on. Hold to your heart and bless it, visualizing golden energy radiating out and permeating it with A-U-M from throat.

6. Purchase wormwood and eucalyptus oils. Keep them away from children and animals as they can be highly poisonous. Use eucalyptus oil or incense to dissolve negative energies that cling to used furniture or clothing you purchase before wearing or using them, or to clean the astral environment of a room (pine and deodar is also effective, as is sandalwood). Use wormwood oil very sparingly upon a small patch of skin over places in your muscles and joints that constantly ache, if you suspect that the cause might be crystallized imperil. Never put more than about one or two square inches of wormwood oil on your body at a time. Do this at night and drink two large glasses of water. At night or the next morning when you urinate, you will be expelling dissolved crystals of imperil. If

you don't drink enough water, you may become constipated with very dry stools, so drink plenty of water.

Closing

Master Jesus said, "*BE YE PERFECT, EVEN AS YOUR FATHER IN HEAVEN IS PERFECT*." One of the goals of the disciple is to become an increasingly better conductor of light. Purification practices help the individual to accomplish this via self-training of the mind, purification of the constitution and habits, and spiritual communion. Thus, we make ourselves a grounding channel for a higher force to operate in the physical. This is part of the sacrificial service of the disciple and as one proves oneself working in this way, then one gradually becomes entrusted with larger and larger services and responsibilities.

The Iliaster meditation practice, Temple study, Esoteric World Service, and the efforts to meet the requirements of modern discipleship powerfully affect the inner life of the disciple over time. When these things are built into the student's life as normal and rhythmic activities, the resulting release of spiritual force and its use creatively will slowly and normally produce the needed adjustments and spiritual evolution proceeds naturally.

If the Temple Purity Practices are kept daily, the Initiate will make fast and efficient progress toward adeptship. These practices must be integrated into the life and kept from now on.

Recommended Books (available at www.WesternEsotericBooks.com)

Bailey, A. (1971). *Education in the new age*. New York: Lucis Publishing Co.

Bailey, A. (1982). *Glamour: A world problem*. New York: Lucis Publishing Company.

Roerich, H. (1980). *AUM*. New York: Agni Yoga Society.

Roerich, H. (1977). *Hierarchy*. New York: Agni Yoga Society.

Roerich, H. (1981). *Letters of Helena Roerich, Volume 2*. New York: Agni Yoga Society.

Saraydarian, T. (1981). *The psyche and psychism*. Arizona: Aquarian Educational Group.

CHAPTER THIRTEEN
GRAIL PRIESTHOOD

Introduction to the Apostolic Succession

The Apostolic Succession is the most ancient spiritual lineage that can be traced through history. It is more ancient than any historically extant Tibetan, Hindu, Buddhist, Chinese or other lineage of Priesthood or discipleship that we know of. It is approximately 2000 years old. Embedded in the lineages are not only the divine Apostolic powers and energies transmitted directly from the Master Jesus by the laying-on of hands, but also 20 centuries of dedicated work of heart, soul, and spirit that all those who labored in the lineages transmitted through their striving and service. It links all those who operate the lineage with their spiritual ancestors.

Apostolic Succession provides a powerful, invisible link to the Master Jesus and becomes a vital source of interior transformation for each ordained person through meditation, dreams, and the Sacraments. It links members of the Temple of the Holy Grail in the sacred chain of spiritual brothers and sisters who have dedicated themselves to the service of the Christ.

A Closer Look at Apostolic Succession

Apostolic Succession is the lineage of ordination originating with the Master Jesus and his Apostles. It is also known as the Priesthood of

Melchizedek (the great universal human priesthood). Christian priesthood began as the Apostolic commission of the inner circle of 12 disciples chosen from a larger circle of 70 by the Master Jesus. Master Jesus placed his hands upon the head of each Apostle and sent them forth into the world even as he himself had been sent, i.e., "As the Father sent Me, so I send you. Then He breathed on them and said, 'Receive the Holy Spirit.'" (John 20: 21-22).

The disciples that Master Jesus ordained to carry on the work that he had carried on were called "Bearers of the Teachings." In the Greek language it became Apostoli—the Apostles. The Apostles, in turn, each trained close disciples on whom they laid hands as their successors, each becoming a link in the Sacred Chain of the Priesthood of Melchizedek.

These sacred orders streamed out into the world in many different traditions because the Apostles went to different places. Thomas went to India. Mark ended up in Egypt; Peter in Antioch and Rome. Historically, the churches that have preserved these lines of succession and lineages have been separate and separated. The Roman Catholic Pope preserves one line of succession. The Greek Orthodox another. The Coptic another and so on.

Although they had each been taught by Master Jesus, the Apostles had been far from uniform in thought and personality. They had many differences of opinion. Because of the great diversity of thought among the early Apostles, it was inevitable that the churches, which grew out of their separate missionary journeys, would differ widely.

For three centuries, the diverse Christian traditions of India, Persia, Syria, Ethiopia, Palestine, Egypt, Greece, Rome and the western Celtic regions developed in native freedom. Thus, from the earliest times, valid lines of Apostolic succession were maintained outside of the Roman jurisdiction.

Consequently, the succession of the Apostles has been kept, unbroken, in many different chains of succession from the hands of Master Jesus, up to the present time, when he laid hands on his students and they laid hands on theirs. Apostolic Succession is the person-to-person, hands upon head transmission of ordination authority that descends from the Master Jesus through his Apostles. It can be transmitted only by Bishops who are historical successors of the Apostles.

The Priesthood of Melchizedek

Master Jesus was not a priest of Judaism. He was not initiated into the Arayin Priesthood or any of the other priesthoods that existed. Rather it is said by the initiate Paul and others that followed that his priesthood was the Priesthood of Melchizedek—the strange figure who appears in the old testament writings to initiate Abraham. So traditionally, in the Christian priesthood when priests are made, it is said, "Thou art a priest forever after the Order of Melchizedek."

Apostolic Succession in the Home Temple

In the nineteenth century, valid lines of Apostolic Succession were transmitted into independent church groups of Europe, England, and America, much to the chagrin of Roman and other church hierarchies. After years of legal battling in ecclesiastical and secular courts, the Catholic and Orthodox churches were forced to recognize the validity of these "irregular" Apostolic orders.

In the early churches, most members of a congregation were ordained into major or minor Apostolic orders. In T:.H:.G:., all Initiates are given conditional licensure as Subdeacons of the Home Temple Priesthood and taught how to use pre-consecrated elements for operating the First Order Empowerment. Thus, each Initiate is able to experience a direct link with the Master Jesus.

Earlier, those accepted into T:.H:.G:. were ordained into the Apostolic Diaconate so they could do a Deacon's Mass and work the Empowerments with pre-consecrated elements. However, now T∴H∴G∴. Initiates are provided with the Subdeacon's license and the minimal training needed to operate the Self-Empowerments. It is recommended, but not required, that Initiates undertake concurrent studies for ordination in the Home Temple Priesthood. Without ordination to the Diaconate, at minimum, Initiates cannot be advanced to the Second Order.

This change was made so that a far better foundation in Priesthood training could be offered through a separate school called the Home Temple. This is a world-wide distance learning seminary for ordination into Apostolic Priesthood. The Grailmaster and Grail Mother are the Presiding Bishops and Directors of the Home Temple (www.HomeTemple.org). All the audio and video tapes as well as the handbook materials for each level of ordination in the Home Temple program have been written and produced by the Grailmaster and Grail Mother.

To the threefold major orders of Bishop, Priest, and Deacon, which are transmitted through ordination and laying-on of hands, we have added the minor-order office of Subdeacon, for which certification from the Presiding Bishops is provided when a person first undertakes studies as a Postulant for ordination as a Deacon. Since the offices of Priest and Deacon are incremental delegations of Apostolic authority by laying-on of hands, the certification as Subdeacon is also such a delegation. It is under this same rubric that T∴H∴G∴. Initiates receive their licenses as Subdeacons that allow them to operate the Self-Empowerments.

Currently, only Home Temple Priests and Priestesses chosen and elected to train as Bishops are required to go through the T∴H∴G∴. First Order Empowerments as part of their Episcopal training. Otherwise, training in the Home Temple Apostolic Priesthood is non-initiatic. It is intended to be an "outer court" to the Temple.

The application and acceptance procedure for T∴H∴G∴. Initiation is exactly the same as admission to studies for ordination in the Home Temple, and it operates under the same standards. Acceptance into either school ensures acceptance into the other.

Normally, T:.H:.G:. Initiates who choose to undertake Home Temple studies can complete ordinations to both Diaconate and Priesthood within thirteen months, or by the time they are finishing the First Order Empowerments. The Liturgist, Root Chakra, and other theurgical Empowerments become far more potent when operated by an Ordained Initiate. That is another reason concurrent studies in each school are recommended.

The Liturgy of the Holy Grail and the Sang Real

We can understand the importance of the Apostolic lineage. But what about Priesthood? Why is there a Priesthood associated with the Temple, and why must Templars perform a theurgical liturgy to facilitate Self-Empowerments?

Central to the operation of the Empowerments is the theurgical and sacramental Liturgy of the Holy Grail, also known as the Liturgy of the Chalice. The Grail Liturgy, symbolized by the flaming chalice, has superficial resemblance to Christian communion services only because the classic medieval Mass was derived from ancient and esoteric mystery liturgies far older than Christianity. But the Liturgy of the Holy Grail is ancient and universal, including not only Christian, but Jewish, Tibetan, Mithraic, Druidic, Zoroastrian, Egyptian, shamanic, and a host of other advanced spiritual practices based upon a sacred meal, priesthood, and divine communion.

The Grailmaster and Temple are Apostolic keepers of the True Grail, which as a spiritual substance is the Eternal *Sang Real* or Divine Royal Blood (*San Greal* in Christian esoteric tradition, "Holy Grail," often confused with the Grail Chalice itself). The Grail is both the Graal Path and the Divine sacrificial energy (normally invisible and intangible) that nurtures evolutionary unfoldment in the physical universe and among beings developing amidst the disharmony, darkness, and chaos of this nethermost plane of existence. In the T∴H∴G∴. Empowerments, it works with spiritual Hierarchy, the Eggregore of the Temple, and sacred lunar cycles to incubate spiritual powers within prepared Initiates.

The Grail Sacrament embodies the power that sanctifies matter, quickening its spiritual vibration and level of refinement. It is the actual substance of Divine Blessing ("sprinkling with sacrificial Blood") or Divine Bliss ("Blood sanctification"), or the Body and Blood of the Christ. It is the Philosopher's Stone, Elixir, or Amritha that transforms the lower into the Higher, expands the crystallized or contracted Heart-consciousness, and mediates inspiration, guidance, selfless service, and Divine Love.

In the Liturgy of the Chalice, the Divine Nectars, Fragrances, and Essences of the Holy Grail are poured out as a potent blessing for the spiritual evolution of all beings in all worlds, and especially for those on this plane of existence. First Order Templars are trained in Theurgical Operations of the Liturgy and daily practice of the Blessing Way, benefiting immensely from these works when carried out with fiery, selfless devotion to humanity, the Divine Will, and all beings.

Through the work of Temple Priesthood, the True Grail is poured out for the sake of the New Humanity and the New World that are coming into manifestation. Made tangible in a Divine Theurgical Sacrament for higher human and planetary Initiation, the potencies of the True Grail are invoked and evoked in sacred Grail Priesthood.

The Grail Sacrament is the lifeblood of the Temple. Those accepted for Initiation are instructed in basic priestly and theurgical operation with consecrated elements. They are encouraged, but not required, to undertake the full Home Temple Priesthood training concurrent with completion of First Order Empowerments. Without ordination into at least the Diaconate, Temple Initiates cannot be Advanced to Second Order.

Closing

The Orders of the Temple are the Apostolic orders of the Master Jesus—the Orders of Melchizedek. The lineage that comes from the Master Jesus is a special, sacred, and esoteric seed that is carried through history, and many times has never been germinated. The time for the germination of that seed is now. The seed does not belong to the past, it belongs to the future.

CHAPTER FOURTEEN
MICROCOSM, MACROCOSM, AND TEACHINGS ON THEURGICAL OPERATIONS

The human soul is a microcosm. That is to say, it is a holograph of the entire universe—visible and invisible—which is known as the macrocosm. The macrocosm is the primordial Image of God, the *Imago Dei,* in which humanity is formed. Plato *Timeaus* and the Hermetic *Kore Kosmou* call the macrocosm the Son of God, the Divine Offspring of God, because it is the emanated and existent aspect of Godhead.

The universe is a pleroma of soul and consciousness streaming forth from Godhead as from a central Fountain. All beings are sentient. Each human soul has been formed from aeons of sacred psychic marriages of lesser mineral, vegetable, and animal souls. Human souls, unlike those of lesser beings, are the result of an archetypal initiatic process of *heiros gamos* on all psychic levels and involving all aspects of the cosmos.

For this reason, each human soul is a microcosm and contains within it the energies, sympathies, and patterns of all sentient beings—i.e., of all that exists in the visible and invisible worlds. Within each human soul are all the ranks of angels and archangels, all the suns, moons, and galaxies, all the subtle bodies of all beings, whether physical, astral, mental, or divine.

Invisible World and Subtle Dimensions

Incarnate human souls live in an inverted Reality. That which is most gross and obvious possesses the least Reality, and that which is most subtle possesses the greatest Reality. We are like fish under water that look upward and see their own reflection. To them, there is nothing beyond the surface of the pond, for the surface acts as a reflective boundary preserving the illusion that all Reality lies below the surface. This is the condition of the philosopher in Plato's Allegory of the Cave, and the condition of all humanity. We are trapped in the illusion of an inverted Reality, where that which is least Real commands our attention and seems to control our lives.

In order to gain perspective, it is important for us to realize that our ordinary perception and consciousness operates on the lowest, most gross level of Reality—the Physical Plane. We operate under the illusion that solid, material, physical Reality is all that exists when, in fact, there are numerous invisible worlds and dimensions around us and within us. These subtle planes of existence are home to myriad forms of life, soul, and consciousness that interpenetrate and affect us unknowingly. Disease, depression, obsession, possession, and madness are some of the ways these forces can negatively affect us. Health, joy, inspiration, and divine communion are other ways they can affect us.

What is more, the invisible Realities include currents of force and consciousness that are mediated through the configurations of stars, planets, and other cosmic entities. The Initiate learns to navigate through both calm and violent waters by using the prevailing currents constructively, rather than allowing them to oppose and ruin all that is attempted. These include not only the chemism of astrological, solar, and lunar cycles, but the tides of prana, the influx of non-cyclic cosmic events, the tatvas, and a host of other currents that only the truly sensitive Initiate can feel and evaluate.

Below is shown a chart of the Lower Planes into which each soul is incarnated, beginning with the familiar physical earth sub-plane and extending inward into the increasingly subtle sub-planes of Physical, Astral, and Mental Reality. Examine this carefully. You will see that "Hell" is not below, but above—in the lower Astral and Mental sub-planes. You will see that the alchemical symbols of earth, water, air, and fire have correspondences in all of the Lower Planes of what we call Reflected or Inverted Reality. You will also see that your physical body has, in addition to its tangible biological organs, quite extensive etheric or radiant electromagnetic and luminous plasmas. They constitute what we call the auric egg or envelope, which extends far beyond your physical skin and interconnects you with even more expanded and subtle aspects of your invisible self.

Constitution of the Human Microcosmic Body

From inverted human perspective looking from the Seventh Plane Physical inward into the depths or upward into the heights of the increasingly subtle mysteries of the Microcosmic Self.

PHYSICAL PLANE

EARTH (solids, archates, trace minerals of
body , bones, teeth, hair, nails, carti1age, and
mesodermal structures)   Sub-Plane 1

WATER (blood plasmas, lymphatic
and glandular secretions, digestive and
other enzymes, and endodermal structures)   Sub-Plane 2

AIR (neural tissues, brain, dissolved
gases in blood and dermal tissues,
and ectodermal structures)   Sub-Plane 3

FIERY CHEMICAL ETHERS OR PLASMAS
(auric "magnetic;" imperil-forming ethers;
interface with pranic ethers from
Sun, stars, and all radiant iliasters mediated
to the physical body)   **Sub-Plane 4**
BASE OF SPINE, GENERATIVE, SOLAR PLEXUS, SPLEEN
                                                          INTERMEDIARY

VITAL ETHERS, PLASMAS, OR PRANAS
(solar, astral, etc., transmitted by conduction or induction)**Sub-Plane 5**
THROAT

LUMINOUS ETHERS OR PLASMAS (light-energies
transmitted by radiation)   **Sub-Plane 6**
HEART

REFLECTIVE ETHERS OR PLASMAS (Logoic "sound"
and mirror-like, akashic iliasters that reflect astral image)   **Sub-Plane 7**
AJNA (to Spleen), CROWN; PHYSICAL PERMANENT ATOM

                                                          ASTRAL PLANE

LOWER, INVERTED ASTRAL PLANES OF SUFFERING:

INFERNAL (demoniacal angelic and elemental,
criminal human;   **Sub-Plane 1**
includes Preterodernal, Infernal, and Proctodernal)
THE HELLS, EARTH ELEMENT

MIDDLE WORLDS   Sub-Plane 2
EMOTIONS, WATER ELEMENT

PASSION WORLDS   Sub-Plane 3
ILLUSION, AIR ELEMENT

INTERMEDIARY ASTRAL PLANE

FIERY REFLECTIVE AND GENERATIVE
SUB-PLANE   Sub-plane 4
BASE OF SPINE, GENERATIVE, SOLAR
PLEXUS, SPLEEN   **INTERMEDIARY**

HIGHER, ANGELIC PLANES OF ASTRAL BLISS:

COSMIC LIQUID SUB-PLANE   Sub-Plane5
THROAT

ASTRAL SUB-PLANE   Sub-Plane 6
HEART

HIGHER PSYCHIC SUB-PLANE   Sub-Plane 7
AJNA (to Spleen), CROWN; ASTRAL PERMANENT ATOM

                                          MENTAL PLANE

INFERNAL MENTAL SUB-PLANE   Sub-Plane 1
(Includes Preterodernal, Infernal, and Proctodernal)

NORMAL MENTAL SUB-PLANE   Sub-Plane 2

INTELLECTUAL MENTAL SUB-PLANE   Sub-Plane 3

INTERMEDIARY MENTAL SUB-PLANE
ILLUMINATED LOWER MIND   Sub-Plane 4
BASE OF SPINE, GENERATIVE,
SOLAR PLEXUS, SPLEEN   INTERMEDIARY

THE CHALICE, LOTUS, HIGHER TRIAD

COSMIC GASEOUS SUB-PLANE   Sub-Plane5
EGOIC LOTUS; SOUL; CAUSAL BODY

NOETIC OR MANASIC SUB-PLANE   Sub-Plane 6
EGOIC LOTUS; SOUL; CAUSAL BODY

HIGHER EGOIC OR "HIGHER SELF"
SUB-PLANE   Sub-Plane 7
EGOIC LOTUS; SOUL; CAUSAL BODY; MENTAL PERMANENT
ATOM

Intermediary Firmament or Boundary Between Lower and Higher Planes

All these worlds are accessible to incarnate beings, for good or for evil. Human adepts can use and manipulate all of the Lower Triad Planes, which are the Microcosmic forces that imitate in manifestation the Realities of the Higher Planes. But the Lower Planes are inverted *reflections* of true Reality, much as the image in a mirror reflects an object. Like a mirror image, everything is backwards. Up is down, and left is right. This is the basic source of illusion in the incarnate state.

Therefore, adepts who exist and operate only in the Lower Triad Planes ultimately succumb to illusion, separatism, egoism, madness, or what might be called "evil." Lacking intimate communion with Spiritual Hierarchy and return to the Higher Planes—in or out of the physical body—self-annihilation and spiritual death is the final result. The entire soul disintegrates and all elements return to the lowest state of Reality in the Eighth Plane of preterodernal, infernal, and proctodernal fires, which like the crude slurries of the potter are the starting places for aeons of re-formation and re-configuration. The remains of such beings will again become active in the Anodos or evolutionary ascent only in the next planetary chain, after the interval known as Pralaya.

Adepts of the Atlantean brotherhoods have operated for tens of thousands of years in the subtle regions of the Lower Triad Planes and subplanes. They live in astral bodies and personalities that normally decay a few weeks or months after death as the essential Monadic being returns to its Higher Planes for reintegration and preparation to reincarnate. However, they have mastered the Egyptian art of prolonging the life of the astral body by drawing vital forces from incarnate humans and animals, so they live for many ages.

Some of them are wise beings who instruct mankind, but because they have not allowed themselves to surrender to death and reintegration, most of them have degenerated into powerful negative forces who have alienated themselves from communion with the Higher Planes and Spiritual Hierarchy. They are allegorized in religion as the fallen angels who have chosen to leave Heaven, or various pantheons of gods.

The Higher Self

The first Higher Plane of Reality beyond the firmament or boundary that separates the Lower Triad from the Higher Worlds is known as the Buddhic or Wisdom Plane. This contains the Manasic or Higher Mental sub-planes and the Heart Consciousness of what has been called the Egoic Lotus or Higher Self, which is symbolized by the Flame in the Chalice.

This correlates to Tiphareth, the spiritual and intuitional intelligence of the Heart Center and the "brain" of the human soul, which is projected as a ray from the Monad or spiritual individuality that, in turn, is projected from Godhead.

The Higher Self can unfold only by the operation of its projection or incarnation into the Lower Triad as a human personality. It is in flesh that the soul is able to grow and develop—through experience in time and space. That is what is allegorized by the dividing of Adam, the primal Human, into two sexes and the expulsion of Adam and Eve from Paradise. The wise Serpent was a manifestation of God setting in motion the great Monadic Journey. It is only through incarnate pain and joy, failure and success, trial and error, that the human soul can become truly pure and divine.

Seeds of Christhood

Humanity is predestined to nurture, develop, and bring to fruition the seed of Christhood planted deep within its Heart. That is the allegory of the lotus rising from the muck of a pond, until it finally breaks the surface of the water and blossoms in the full light of the sun. In Eastern philosophy the Higher Self is compared to the lotus, which puts out petals—each petal a manifestation of divine Reality: Knowledge, Love, etc. When finally the petals fall away leaving the naked heart of the lotus containing seed for the next generation, the cycle is complete. Thus, the Petals of the Egoic Lotus fall away when the human soul becomes a fully developed Great Soul or *Mahatma*, and the Self becomes one with the Monad that projected it.

In the West we use an alchemical allegory based upon the retort and the alchemical vessel or chalice. In Gnostic and Kabbalistic allegory, the divine spark in every Heart can never be quenched, and eventually will blaze like a bonfire. The Chalice is analogous to the Lotus as the region of the Lower and Higher Triad that contains the Higher Self. The firmament or boundary between Higher and Lower worlds of the Chalice—the Lower Macrocosm and Higher Microcosm—becomes a friendly interface for incarnate saints, who experience divine communion and guidance while yet in flesh.

The Chalice is the vessel that collects and stores the *iliaster* or *akasha* of all human and previous incarnate experience. This is transmitted unconsciously from incarnation to incarnation in the progress and building of the soul. To illustrate, simply because a person spoke French in a previous lifetime, it doesn't mean his or her next incarnate personality in an English-speaking culture will be able to speak French without studying it. However, it does mean that the new personality will find an affinity for the French language and be able to learn it easily.

One way Templars learn about previous incarnations is through a study of affinities and an analysis of patterns in the individual ontogeny or life-development. This is done in the Antahkarana Building Empowerment. However, the first way Templars learn about their previous transmigrations in mineral, vegetable, animal, and human kingdoms is through the work of the Initiatic Vigil, which is done on or near the Easter-Passover Full Moon, as discussed in the final chapter of this book.

The Development of a New Master

In alchemical allegory, we say that a time comes when the human soul approaches the culmination of its development. Continuity of consciousness is established with the Higher Self, and the need for incarnation becomes less and less. Then we say that the tiers of the Chalice burn and melt away, until finally all that remains on the stem of the Chalice is the Philosopher's Stone—the Higher Self. All incarnations of the soul have been gathered together in one sacred marriage to produce a Great Soul or

Master, who now has no need of incarnation and becomes one with Spiritual Hierarchy.

Such a being has graduated from the Human Kingdom and may appear to us as an impersonal being. But, in fact, the new Master is far more highly individuated than any human personality, far more capable of universal love, far wiser and more intelligent, and far more creative than we can imagine. We can no longer use the terms "he" or "she," since this being is androgynous like the angels. "It" is not a good term, either. Perhaps "they" is the most accurate pronoun.

They may choose to assist mankind by manifesting in an illusory or temporary body, walking anonymously among humanity, or even undertaking rebirth in a human womb to "re-member" or reconstruct themselves as they mature. Or they may operate telepathically by generating higher creative emotional and intellectual forces that sensitive human souls can sense as inspiration, joy, and bliss. They may overshadow or "overlight" composers, writers, and teachers.

The Hands and Fingers of God

It is vital to develop and keep faith with Spiritual Hierarchy, who are the Masters and Guides of humanity—our Elder Brother-Sisters in Spirit. It is they who rescue us from the dark, negative, devolutionary, and antihumanistic forces mankind has generated and continues to generate on the Earth. It is they who serve as unseen channels of inspiration, invention, and creativity for all humanity. It is from their ranks that all the great teachers and avatars of history have appeared on Earth to instruct and redeem mankind from its natural self-pollution and the other necessary debris of life-experience on Earth. We should always reverence them as the hands and fingers of God.

The Temple of the Holy Grail was established and continues to be guided by Spiritual Hierarchy. Under the Master Jesus, the Master

Hilarion has been especially active with T∴H∴G∴. Other masters who developed from ancient Gnostic, Hermetic, Kabbalistic, Templar, Rosicrucian, and Theosophical saints are also active in the Eggregore of the Temple.

Initiatic Theurgical Operations

When some magicians draw their magic circles and uses symbols, formulas, and substances to evoke and command supposed angelic beings, they are projecting a grand illusion. Little do they know that whatever effect they see is not external, but internal. That is why one who tries to practice from the medieval grimoires soon find themselves overwhelmed from within and on the edge of madness. He or she has played ignorantly with the fiery forces of the Divine Microcosm and radically disturbed the internal boundaries of their soul.

True spiritual adepts work in the Lower Triad Planes through theurgical operation under the direct guidance of Spiritual Hierarchy. Temple Initiates learn to operate theurgically for blessing, healing, protection, and other constructive invisible service. The Temple operations have been so designed that it is impossible to abuse them. These arts are taught in First Empowerment, Root Chakra, Healing, Long-Life, Antahkarana-Building, and Liturgist Empowerments. They are done through use of the Temple Talisman, the Grail Liturgy, the Long-Life Stone, and other resources.

The genuine adept stills the storm or brings rain not by invoking external sources, but through an intimate process of interior communication and control. He or she communicates with animals and other non-human beings primarily from within the Heart, and only secondarily through the medium of voice, sound, or movement.

The Temple Initiate studies the harmony of the internal and external worlds, engaging in constructive exercises to develop the subtle forces of the microcosm. In the Root Chakra Empowerment, which is begun as soon as the First Empowerment over Dark Force has been accomplished, the Initiate undertakes a series of experiments and exercises that will eventually allow safe communication with elemental beings and effective theurgical operation for constructive purposes from within the Eggregore of the Temple. After the passing of a full solar cycle or one year, if the work of Root Chakra has been faithfully followed, he or she will be able to demonstrate abilities to affect weather and other elemental forces. In the Liturgist Empowerment, he or she will be able to demonstrate other forms of creative manifestation, healing, and constructive theurgical operation.

Earth as Paradise

An age may come in which all humanity will develop the sensibilities we associate with adeptship, but as part of ordinary consciousness and perception. In that age the Earth will be a Paradise, and there will be no enmity between mankind and nature. We will no longer live amidst tons of concrete and atmospheric pollution, but in gardens and forests. We will not cut and kill trees to make our homes, but grow them. When a new child is born, he or she will be given a sacred grove of trees that will become friendly allies and over the years that will grow into his or her adult home and shelter.

People will live incarnate in their bodies for hundreds of years. What computers and telephony do today will be done by human minds and telepathic communication. There will be very little machinery as we know it today, and people will travel both astrally and physically by means of projection and use of the Earth's magnetic currents. People will live and be conscious on all of the Lower Triad Planes.

CHAPTER FIFTEEN
VIGIL, TEMPLE INITIATION, AND EMPOWERMENTS

The Temple of the Holy Grail is an Initiatic Mystery School for mature women and men who feel ready to privately undertake advanced esoteric spiritual training in order to anonymously serve human and planetary evolution. The purpose of T∴H∴G∴ is to empower people dedicated to a life of service. There is no discrimination by sex, age, race, or sexual orientation. However, in their application form, candidates for Initiation must demonstrate evidence of dedication and achievement in human service. They must also provide personal references who can vouch for their character and motivation.

Overview of Admission and the Initiatic Process

All fields of endeavor have sacred dimensions that Grail Teachings, Sacraments, and Empowerments can potentiate and inspire. Admission to the Initiatic process and First Order Empowerments opens new dimensions of effective and invisible service in all fields, whether professional, artistic, medical, educational, religious, commercial, social, domestic, or manual labor.

Wesak Initiation

Initiation into the Temple of the Holy Grail is done once each year at the exact time of the Wesak Full Moon, which for T∴H∴G∴ is the full moon following the Easter-Passover Moon and is sometimes in variance with the Buddhist date for Wesak. It is done by Spiritual Hierarchy in cooperation with the Grailmaster and Grail Mother, the Synod of Bishops Templar, and the individual Initiand, or Candidate for Initiation.

Each Initiand must have:

- completed the Probationary Studies (as given in this book and supplementary tapes)

- developed Temple Meditation for the evocation of Iliaster or Christ Light

- successfully completed the work of the Initiatic Vigil

- completed the Vigil Analysis

- been trained, authorized, and supplied with the sacred materials and consecrated elements for private Wesak Self-Initiation and First Empowerment.

During the ritual of the Wesak Self-Initiation, the Temple Talisman of the new Initiate is activated and he or she consecrates a violet length of yarn for the Necklace Practice. The coming month will be devoted to this practice and the First Empowerment Studies.

Without formal training and acceptance for Initiation, a person cannot receive the Initiation. Without the Initiation, regardless of what materials, texts, tapes, and supplies a person may have obtained, it is not possible to receive the First Order Empowerments. Finally, it is not possible for any Initiate or non-Initiate to misuse or abuse the theurgical operations of the Grail Sacrament and Rites. All of these conditions have been established in the Eggregore of the Temple.

The Initiatic Vigil is an all-night work that may be done any night from three days (72 hours) before the exact time of the Easter-Passover Full

Moon to three days after. Wesak Initiation, one month later, does not have this flexibility. It must be coordinated with the *exact time* of the Full Wesak Moon, which could be any hour of the day or night, on any day of the week. Therefore the Initiand must be prepared to set up for private ritual whenever required—perhaps at 3:12 A.M. in the wee hours of a Tuesday, or at 1:46 P.M. on a Friday afternoon. He or she will have to make arrangements for this. The total time required is about an hour, with the ritual work commencing about half an hour before the time of the exact full moon.

Progress through the First Order Empowerments

When the First Empowerment has been completed, the Initiate will request and receive sacramental materials, tapes, written studies, and practices for the first part of Root Chakra Empowerment and the Long-Life Empowerment. Like the Initiation, these will be done with a combination of daily practices and special sacramental work at the exact times of new and full moons. The time of the actual Empowerment ritual depends upon the moon. The Initiate must prepare to have privacy for sacramental work at these times.

When the Long-Life Empowerment has been received and established, he or she will request and receive sacramental materials, tapes, written studies, and practices for Heart of the Master and Healer Empowerments. After these have been completed, the Initiate will request and receive sacramental materials, tapes, written studies, and practices for the Liturgist Empowerment including the final parts of Root Chakra Empowerment, as well as the Certificate of acceptance as a Companion in the Chivalric Order +OMR+.

Then he or she will work personally with the Grailmaster by telephone, fax, postal mail, and/or e-mail to document and accomplish the theurgical operation with elemental spirits. When success has been demonstrated, both Empowerments will have been received.

Before the Easter-Wesak season of the year following Initiation, the Initiate will request and receive sacred materials, tapes, written studies, and practices for the Antahkarana Building Empowerment, which must be done in coordination with the Wesak moon cycles. It is not necessary to have completed all or most of the other Empowerments in order to do this one, which can be done only during this season.

When all seven of the First Order Empowerment have been completed, the Initiate may request dubbing as a Dame or Knight of the +OMR+ by the Grailmaster at their mutual convenience. Many Initiates combine this with ordination into Home Temple Priesthood or Episcopate, if they have done concurrent Priesthood training.

Summary of First Order Empowerments

FIRST EMPOWERMENT: Empowerment over Dark Forces, (Two consecutive Full Moons). *Materials for First Empowerment are sent with Wesak Initiation Package.*

ROOT CHAKRA EMPOWERMENT, Part One: Practices and work with Elementals and the Blessing Way (introduced concurrent with Long-Life Empowerment).

LONG-LIFE EMPOWERMENT: (One New-Moon cycle) *Materials sent after First Empowerment has been completed.*

HEART OF THE MASTER EMPOWERMENT: or Initiation as Chela of Master Jesus (Two consecutive Full Moons).

HEALER EMPOWERMENT: Work with cells and Elementaries; Acceptance as Companion of +OMR+ (One New-Moon Cycle). *Materials sent after Long-Life Empowerment has been completed.*

ANTAHKARANA-BUILDING EMPOWERMENT: Preparation for completion of First-Order Empowerments and Dubbing as Knight or Dame in +OMR+ (Easter Full Moon to Wesak Full Moon). *Materials sent in time for Easter-Wesak moons one year after Initiation.*

LITURGIST or SEVENTH EMPOWERMENT: Advanced training in Harmonic Intonation, Mudra, Theurgical Operation, and Grail Sacramental Liturgy (One New-Moon Cycle) with concurrent completion of ROOT CHAKRA EMPOWERMENT (After full solar year of practices; done on Full Moon). *Materials sent including Certificate of Acceptance as Companion in +OMR+ after successful completion of Healer Empowerment. The Seventh or Liturgist Empowerment requires communication and documentation of theurgical operation under personal supervision of Grailmaster.*

Advancement to Second Order

Prerequisite: Apostolic Ordination

The prerequisite for Advancement to Second Order is Apostolic Ordination. An Initiate must hold valid ordination, minimally to the Diaconate, in the Home Temple or other Apostolic lineages.

He or she may also request advancement into the Second Order to undertake the Christ-Melchizedek Generation and Completion Stage Practices. This will require the Portal Preparations, Studies, and Practices and the C-Day Vault Initiation, which can be done only in person by the Grailmaster. Candidates must come at their own expense for this

Advancement and bear their share of the costs. The Generation and Completion Stage Practices will require long-term and ongoing instruction.

Summary of Second Order Empowerments

PORTAL TO SECOND ORDER: Studies, tapes, and practices done over at least ten weeks during the 100 days between the March Equinox and C-Day. *Materials sent before March 21.*

VAULT INITIATION INTO SECOND ORDER: Done on or about July 1st with Grailmaster and Grail Mother; requires travel and sharing of Initiation expenses. This confers:

GRAIL PRIEST/PRIESTESS ADEPTUS MINOR Grade of 5=6 (Tiphareth): (Advancement and Initiation into the practice of Generation and Completion Stages of the Melchizedekian Tantra. Development of Androgynous Melchizedek Enthroned). Second Order Templars do all Kabbalistic advancements from Tiphareth, as that is the Central Channel and Middle Pillar upon which they must dwell to create and achieve the Work of Da'ath. However, they do advance by extension to higher grades that are referred by Paths to Tiphareth (6=5 through a potential 10=1). *Material received at Initiation consists of Melchizedekian Generation Stages I-II tapes, videotape, study materials, and practices, and E-mail and/or telephone guidance by Grailmaster or Grail Mother.*

GRAIL PRIEST/PRIESTESS ADEPTUS MAJOR, Grade of 6=5 (Geburah): (Development of microcosmic winds, channels, and paths to the Heart). *Materials sent consist of Generation Stages III-IV tapes, study materials, and practices, and E-mail and/or telephone guidance by Grailmaster or Grail Mother.*

GRAIL MAGUS/MAGA, Grade of 7=4 (Hesed): (Control of winds, channels, and paths to Heart Development of microcosmic powers in Divine Service. Lucid sleep expands into twenty-four hour continuum of conscious, intentional service. Projection in the Astrum. Completion of the Melchizedek Mandala with ability to unfold every detail in a three-hour meditation). *Materials sent consist of Generation Stages V-VII tapes, study materials, practices, and E-mail and/or telephone guidance by Grailmaster or Grail Mother.*

GRAIL KING/QUEEN, Grade of 8=3 (Da'ath-Binah): (Death practices to attain the Fourth Iliaster). *Materials sent consist of Completion Stage I tapes, study materials, practices, and E-mail and/or telephone guidance by Grailmaster or Grail Mother.*

APPRENTICE OF THE CHRIST, Grade of 9=2 (Da'ath-Hochmah): (Practices to create the Resurrection Body of the Fourth Iliaster). *Materials sent consist of Completion Stage II tapes, study materials, and practices which must be realized in isolation from any human guidance. Minimal contact with Grailmaster or Grail Mother. Specialized telepathic guidance by Christed Masters.*

MASTER, Grade of 10=1 (Da'ath-Kether): (Ipsissima; Christ; Buddha): (*Initiation into Third Order and Spiritual Hierarchy by Invisible Christed Masters). Stage of No Practice and Continual Divine Communion.*

Closing

The Temple of the Holy Grail now stands fully operational as a vessel to serve the New Humanity, as a repository of initiatic wisdom both old and new, and as a powerful Mystery School for the 21st century.

We invite you to apply.

APPENDIX 1
APPLICATION FOR INITIATION

Complete and Mail to:
THG
+GM+
P.O. BOX 3816
SANTA CRUZ, CA 95003-3816
U.S.A.

Statement of Non-Discrimination

T:.H:.G:. Initiation and First Order Empowerments are open to all sincere aspirants with a high school education or the equivalent skills. The Temple does not discriminate against applicants on the basis of race, gender, age, sexual orientation, or previous criminal history. However, applicants must answer all screening questions and provide the names, addresses, and telephone numbers of three personal references. At the discretion of the Grailmaster or Grail Mother, an applicant may be required to complete a psychological screening consisting of multiple-choice responses to twenty statements, and to call for a telephone interview.

The Grailmaster and Grail Mother reserve the right to deny applications from individuals who, in their judgment, are not suited for Temple training based upon psychological, moral, maturational, or other criteria.

T:.H:.G:. Data Base Information

Full Name:
Mailing Address:

Home Telephone:
Work Telephone:
E-Mail Address:
Fax Number:
Date and Place of Birth:
Type of Computer (circle one):   PC MAC
Word Processing Program (circle):   WORD CLARIS
OTHER (Name):

Education (circle highest level completed):
HIGH SCHOOL   COMMUNITY COL-
LEGE
COLLEGE/UNIVERSITY   GRADUATE SCHOOL

Academic and Professional Degrees and Licenses (list):

What is your current work or profession?

Brief Essay Questions (Please *hand* write in the space below)

1. What is your motivation for seeking the Initiation and Empowerments?

2. What are your current spiritual practices and religious affiliations?

3. How do you currently serve in society, and what are your ideals about service? (This includes parenthood, teaching, the arts, politics—all the ways you contact others in service).

4. Briefly describe your religious, theological, moral, or other spiritual beliefs or opinions.

5. If you have a resume or C.V., please attach a copy of it to this application.

Health and Special Conditions
(Please answer all questions that apply to you)

1. Do you have any special needs that our program can try to accommodate (dyslexia, deafness, blindness, etc.)? If so, how can we work with you in specific problem areas?

2. What health problems do you have (if any), and how do you deal with them?

3. Which of the following do you use (if any), and to what degree?

Tobacco	(Circle one) Light Moderate Heavy
Alcohol	(Circle one) Light Moderate Heavy
Recreational Drugs	(Circle one) Light Moderate Heavy

4. Do you have emotional or physical problems, addictions, or behaviors that you are you trying to overcome? Are you in psychological counseling? Explain.

5. If you are a prison inmate, do you have free access to correspondence materials as well as access to audio and video cassette players? Explain your current circumstances.

6. If you have previously received Apostolic Succession from a valid Bishop, please attach a separate page to describe the office you currently hold (Deacon, Priest, Bishop), by whom you were ordained and when, and your current relationship with him or her.

PERSONAL REFERENCES

Please list the names, mailing addresses, and telephone numbers of three people who know you well and would be willing to provide a character recommendation for you:

Name:
Address:

Telephone:

Name:
Address:

Telephone:

Name:
Address:

Telephone:

ADDITIONAL BOOKS BY +GM+

RECOMMENDED FOR APPLICANTS TO THE TEMPLE OF THE HOLY GRAIL

These titles may be ordered directly from the Home Temple Press at *http://www.hometemple.org* or by telephoning the Home Temple at 1-800-909-7069 Pin Code #00

Astral man to Cosmic Christ

Novel *The Astral Man* written by Keizer in 1975 was revised in 1999 in partnership with Eugene E. Whitworth, author of *The Nine Faces of Christ* and many other esoteric novels. Woven into the adventure of a young man recruited to train as a psychic spy for the U.S. military are hundreds of esoteric hints and spiritual clues for those able to recognize them.

Harmonic intoning and chanting: Instruction, technique, and esoteric principles

Includes cassette tapes coordinated with the text to give detailed instruction and practice in harmonic chanting and intoning. *Strongly recommended.*

Initiation: Ancient and modern

Analyzes the meaning and methodology of Initiation with detailed examinations of shamanic, Osirian, Eleusinian, Hermetic, and other mystery schools, categorizing the Grade One Initiations mentioned, (but not discussed) in Alice Bailey's book *Initiation: Human and Solar.*

Keys of the Master: Aramaic key words and Divine concepts in the authentic historical teaching of the Master Jesus

The basic textbook used in the Home Temple Priesthood Studies for developing the introduction gained in *The Authentic Jesus*. Encyclopedic alphabetical listing of basic concepts and words spoken in Aramaic and Hebrew by the Master Jesus, with detailed interpretations. *Strongly recommended.*

Mother Jennie's garden

The autobiography of Dr. Keizer's teacher, Mother Jennie, as told by her in many hours of taped interview. Keizer's tribute to his remarkable teacher and beloved friend, who passed out of her body in 1975 at the age of 97 years.

Priesthood in the new age

The development of universal lay or non-professional Apostolic Priesthood in present and future times is related to its many precursor movements and to the historical background of contemporary spiritual developments contributing to the Home Temple movement.

Prophecies concerning the new church

The prophecies of Nostradamus and other Western mystics about the future of esoteric Christianity are translated, examined, and analyzed. Insights into twenty-first century world spiritual events.

Sepher Ha-Razim and its tradition: An inquiry into the interrelation of Jewish, Greco-Egyptian, and Chaldean magico-mystic practices in the Roman-Hellenistic period

Investigations into magical and Gnostic theurgical traditions contemporary with Jesus. Margalioth's reconstructed book of Hebrew

Kabbalistic magic is examined along with portions of the Greek Magical Papyri, the *Mithrisliturgie,* and other significant sources.

The authentic Jesus: A guide to Aramaic idioms, recent research, and the original message of Jesus Christ

The basic textbook used in the Home Temple Diaconate Studies for introducing the historic background and teachings of the Master Jesus. Based upon Aramaic language concepts and the background of historical Jewish mysticism without which the teachings cannot be understood. Originally written in 1976 and revised in 1998, this book anticipated the work and many of the conclusions of the controversial Jesus Seminar—an ecumenical research project of scholars to recover the historical teachings of Jesus. Keizer's understanding and evaluation of the sources, however, represents a more profound and constructive spiritual understanding than was achieved in most publications of the Jesus Seminar, many of which focused upon merely debunking Christian theology. *Strongly recommended.*

The Gnostic Jesus

PowerPoint lectures on CD-ROM (available soon).

The gospel of Jesus Christ: The simple words of the Master Jesus

Keizer's inspired translation and paraphrase of the teachings of Master Jesus following the Marcan Gospel order and amplified by all extant historical *logia* of Jesus from canonical and non-canonical sources. Clarifies one level of spiritual meaning for non-scholars that is otherwise inaccessible from standard Bible translations, as it is based on original Aramaic language studies and the historical Jewish mysticism and setting out of which Jesus taught. Used as a Lectionary for Home Temple Liturgy of the Chalice. *Strongly recommended.*

The Hermetic sciences: Alchemy, astrology, and kabbalistic theurgy
PowerPoint lectures on CD-ROM (available soon).

The wandering Bishops: Heralds of a new spirituality, second edition
Greatly expanded and rewritten version of the original monograph published in limited edition in 1976. Used in Priesthood Studies of the Home Temple. Overview of Apostolic Succession and the history of the *Episcopi Vagantes* or Independent Bishops leading to the Home Temple and other valid lineages. The clandestine Gnostic and Templar successions of Europe, the Order of Corporate Reunion, the transplanting of Orthodox and other non-Roman Catholic Episcopal lineages to America, independent Bishops win secular and canonical court battles for validity, the Theosophical lineages, the Consecration of women Bishops in Canada, the U.S., and worldwide. Two chapters of Bishop Keizer's memoirs and biographies of significant twentieth-century "Apostles of a New Age." Many photographs.

The western mystery tradition, ancient and modern
PowerPoint lectures on CD-ROM (available soon).

TEMPLE VOCABULARY

Read through these definitions. Many are used in written and recorded instructions.

PARACELSIAN PHENOMENAL REALITIES

ADROP, AZANE, AZAR

Philosopher's Stone; Essential principle of *Sang Real.*

AZOTH

The Astral Light or *Ain Soph Aur,* vehicle of universal life-essence, which in gross aspect is the electrical potential found in air through ozone and oxygen compounds.

BERYLLUS

Magic mirror or crystal in whose Astral aura the clairvoyant may see apparitions. *Berillistica ars:* the art of divination by making the mind passive and receptive through fixing the eyes upon flowing water, mirror, cup, chalice, stone, fire in order to receive impressions from the Astral Light.

CHAOMANTIA

Divination by aerial visions in fog, heat, clouds, vapors.

CLISSUS

Life-Force in all things which causes them to grow, flower, and reproduce

EDELPHUS

One who divines from elements of fire, air, water, or earth.

ELECTRUM MAGICUM
Alloy or composition of seven planetary metals made under specific astral currents for magical use; an alloy of great power from which magical tools, rings, mirrors, etc., may be made; Tibetan singing prayer bowl.

ERODINIUM
Vision or symbolic dream of three types: 1.) physiologically caused; 2.) psychologically caused and/or by astral influence; 3.) spiritually caused. The latter is clearly remembered and most significant, but the former can be interpreted with skill. Dreams are called SOMNIA, as well as the astral forces one person may project in sleep—consciously, subconsciously, or superconsciously.

GAMATHEI, GAMAHEU
Stones impressed with magical powers either by nature or through inscribed characters.

ILECH
A union of great power: *Ilech primum, Ileias, Ileadus,* the first beginning, primordial power, first cause; *Ilech supernaturale,* union of higher and lower astral forces; *Ilech magnum,* healing or "wholing" power of medicine working in a living being; *Ilech crudum,* the unification of a body out of its three constituent principles (salt, sulphur, mercury [body, soul, spirit], respectively earth, water, and fire).

ILEIADES
Element of air; the vital principle inbreathed by God into Adam; exsufflation of magus.

ILIASTER. YLIASTER
Prima materia, akasha, the hidden essence in nature by which all things grow and multiply; *Riaster primus,* life-essence; *Iliaster secundus,* power of life inherent in nature; *Iliaster terius,* astral power of humankind; *Iliaster quartus,* perfection, the power obtained by squaring the circle.

IMPRESSIONS
Effects of passive or receptive imagination caused by astral or other sub-liminal and hypnotic suggestions or influences. Can give rise to disease, psychosomatic symptoms, and even hysterical symptoms.

MATRICES
The elementary vehicles of things.

MUMIA
The life-essence (*jiva,* vital force) contained in a physical vehicle such as parts of animal and vegetable bodies, menstrual blood, semen, hair, fin-gernails, etc., through which the donor organisms may be affected for as long as the mumia is fresh and not yet escaped from the vehicle. May also be used to imprint an aquastor for white or black magical purposes.

MYSTERIUM MAGNUM
Ultimate essence of all matter, *Parabrahman;* God as Chaos.

NECROMANTIA, NIGERMANTIA, BLACK MAGIC
Abuse of occult power and practical knowledge.

NECTROMANTIA
Clairvoyance, clairaudience, psychometry, straight-knowledge, intu-ition, higher discrimination of intentions and meanings—all clear percep-tion of the interiors of things.

PENTACULA
Metallic plates engraved with magical symbols and polarized with will and mind.

SPIRITUS VITAE, VITAL FORCE, PRANA
Principle drawn from elements of whatever serves as the nutrient, and which may be imparted by "magnetism" using olive oil or other media; used for certain kinds of healing.

TERAPH, TERAPHIM
Material form used as a control, telegraph, and intermediary between magus and densified astral body created through will and imagination.

TRARAMES
Invisible initiatic and evolutionary power that communicates with humans through sounds, voices, ringing bells, thunders and other noises.

PARACELSIAN ELEMENTAL AND ASTRAL REALITIES
These include "etheric" and "sidereal" categories

ACTHNA
Invisible, subterrestrial fire associated with bituminous matter and volcanoes; a state of Earth-Soul, being a mixture of material and astral elements.

ACTHNICI
Elemental spirits of fire that may appear as fiery tongues, balls of fire or ground lightning, etc.

ALCOL, EVESTRUM
The substance of a body purified from all physical matter; the etheric "double" or astral body, which can be projected safely as long as the "silver cord" is not broken. The Egyptian "ba." The vehicle for astral travel and the lucid "night work."

ANIADA
Activities caused by astral influence; activity of the subjective imagination.

ANYODEI
Devachan; the subjective state into which the higher essence or Spiritual Principle (Spirit) of the human soul passes after having separated from the animal soul, which is left behind in *Kama Loka*.

AQUASTOR
A being created by the concentration of willed imagination (thought) upon the akashic ether (pure consciousness, Rigpa), by which an ethereal form or body may be created. This can then be animated or given an animal soul (*anima*) by the creator. In theosophical language, a thought-form can become the subtle body for an elemental, succubus, incubus, vampire, or any other class of animal spirit that exists as part of the operator or creator soul and can be projected into form, at times becoming visible and tangible. An EGREGOR is a collective aquastor.

ARCHATES, ARCHALLES
Basic element of the mineral kingdom.

ASTRUM, ASTRAL LIGHT
Higher and universal archaeus of the akasha—the subtlest field of all mind that substands all. It exists more densely around centers of consciousness, chakras, spinal cord, etc., and substands every aura of every sort of being, as well as interconnecting all hearts or centers of beingness.

BRUTA

Psychic forces in animals (associated with human solar plexus); power of animals to instinctively discover curative plants and herbs.

CORPUS INVISIBLE, ETHERIC BODY

Animal soul or *Kama rupa*; lower astral or etheric body

ELEMENTS

Invisible basic principles of all substances solid (earthy), liquid (watery), gaseous (airy), or plasmic (fiery). An ELEMENTARY is an astral corpse of an incarnate being who has biologically died. The corpse will decompose into astral elements, parallel to the decay of a physical body. Elementaries may be galvanized back to life and consciousness. These *abessi* are used as masks by ELEMENTALS, or nature spirits of earth, water, air, and fire [gnomes, salamanders, etc.] many of whom are inverted or "evil," to play with and mislead gullible "channels," mediums, ignorant users of Ouija boards, practitioners of automatic writing, and all who make themselves subjective tools of unseen lower astral forces or supposed "masters" to whom they loan their bodies and voices to deliver what passes for divine wisdom, but is really infernal entrapment, for the "medium" is in fact obsessed and has given away his or her own incarnate integrity, becoming the plaything and slave of inferior, sub-human astral masters. The ELEMENTARIES of more developed souls dissolve quickly, but those of murderers, suicides, and contracted, earth-bound personalities who have died before their time decompose slowly and maintain life and consciousness until the time comes for the division of their principles (full dissolution). These ELEMENTARIES can be dangerous to even somewhat accomplished occultists.

CATEGORIES OF ELEMENTALS AND ASTRAL BEINGS

CABALLI, CABALES, LEMURES
Astral bodies of people who died prematurely by murder or suicide (human will, as opposed to divine will) and live out natural life-term on astral plane (*Kama loca*, earth-bound). These may include certain aborted fetuses and stillborn babies, who live out their terms in parallel lives invisibly with their parents.

CUBITALI, FAERIES, CHANGLINGS, GNOMES, PYGMIES or DWARFS,
Very small elementals of earth in human form with power to change shape. The first four are earth elementals living in the Earth's interior. The Pygmies or Dwarfs carry on endless war with the Gnomes, which to them are giants.

DURDALES, DRYADES
Elementals living in and with trees.

GIGANTES, GIANTS
Elementals of human form but huge size. They are mortal and live like human beings on an astral plane. Called Titans and Nephilim in Greek and Hebrew legend.

GNOMES
Elementals of earth in human-like form. They live, breathe, and walk through rock-solids just as humans do in air.

HOMUNCULI
Artificially made human beings generated from seminal or menstrual fluids as aquastors.

INCUBI AND SUCCUBI

Male and female astral sexual parasites created by vivid imagination coupled with strong sexual lust in masturbation. Elementaries (caballi or the recently died and not yet separated astral cadavers) may be sucked into the parasitic forms during masturbation for carnal intercourse, or witches and sorcerers may astrally visit and attempt sexual intercourse with certain intended victims during sleep.

LEMURES

Elementals of air, including elementaries of deceased humans; causes of "rapping and table tipping" spiritualistic phenomena.

MELUSINAE, UNDINES, ONDINES

Elemental spirits of water, usually appearing in female forms but may also appear as mermaids, fishes, or snakes. Have animal souls like all elementals, but may obtain the divine Spiritual Principle by entering into a marriage or other spiritual union with a male human (fourth principle uniting with fifth). True form is human.

MONSTRA, MONSTERS

Frightening unnatural and demonic beings created from unnatural sexual union of humans and animals or putrefaction of seminal and menstrual fluids galvanized by strong imagination and fear. Today's movies and video images are filling space with monsters and demonic thought-forms that the Black Lodge uses to destroy human and planetary spiritual evolution.

NENUFARENI, SYLPHS

Elementals of air.

NYMPHS
Elementals of water-plants.

PENATES, PENNATES, LARES HERCII, ETESII, MEILICHII, ACTHNICI
Elementals of fire often known as IMPS, HOBGOBLINS, POLTER-GEISTS, and associated with specific locations, haunted houses.

PHANTASMS, GHOSTS, THOUGHT-FORMS
Non-specific "spirits" in solitary places or psychic "events" like the re-running of a movie of a suicide. Often left as a strong psychic impression after a murder, suicide, battle, or in lunatic asylums or solitary confinement cells of a prison, etc.

PYGMIES, DWARFS
Elementals of earth of human shape and microscopic size eternally at war with the Gnomes—not unlike the battle between humans and microbes.

SAGANI
General term for elementals.

SALAMANDERS
Elemental spirits of fire.

SYLPHES
Elementals living in mountainous regions.

SYLVESTRES, DUSII, FAUNS
Elementals living in forests.

SYRENES
Singing melusinae in half human, half fish form, always in water.

UMBRATILES, SHADOWS, WRAITHS
The "etheric double" or *Doppelgaenger* of a physical medium can provide "ectoplasm" or dense astral matter that can be used to temporarily clothe and vitalize lower *astral* of all sorts—usually astral cadavers or "shells," which can be vitalized just as a magnetic tape can be replayed by machine long after the live performance has ceased.

XENI NEPHIDEI
Elemental spirits that give humans power over visible matter and manifestation while feeding on their glands and brains to cause illness and insanity, as in the case of many physical mediums; the "devils" who compact with humans to give them power in exchange for a share in their Divine Principle, to the great detriment of the human agent.

SANSKRIT AND THEOSOPHICAL

AKASHA
The Iliaster out of which all that manifests in form condenses, and into which it may be dissolved by reversal of polarity.

AVITCHI
The Eighth World, Planet of Death, "Hell," eternal cosmic-alchemical fires, whose gateway is the proctodernal or lowest of the astral infernal states. Utter destruction of an astral-etheric form that is totally "wicked" or disharmonious—unable to hold its state but is decaying on the devolutionary arc—occurs in Avitchi. It is reduced to its absolute microcosmic elements which then begin the evolutionary ascent through aeons of time and world-chains.

BARDO

The after-death state into which the human "soul" or consciousness comes, consisting of three stages: existence as an ego in Kama Loka or the astral worlds—abode of the elementaries; the gestation stage after death from Kama Loka; rebirth into the Rupa Loka of Devachan.

DEVACHAN (DEVA-CHAN)

State of human "souls" whose Fifth Principles have been purified and are able to join in the triad of higher principles. They dream in a *maya* of individually and self-generated illusions, during which they review their personal lives and synthesize, harmonize, and stabilize their Individuality before losing all or most memory and being reincarnated on earth or some other kind of world.

GESTATION

The period preceding birth into Devachan after death from the Kama Loka, or preceding incarnation from Devachan.

IMPERIL

Proctodernal mental-astral-etheric negative essence or "irritation" transmissible through sound, rhythm, touch, projected sight that can penetrate the aura and form as black, fiery crystals that pollute the four ethers of a physical body eventually causing mental-emotional irritation (anger, hatred, fear, stress, etc.) and physical disease. Dissolved by water, sterilizing breath, projected blessing, and on physical level (once actually in the aura) by carefully administered wormwood in combination with lavender and eucalyptus oils (as in Temple Soap) used with sound-light practices. Imperil is generated within our auras whenever we qualify hatred, anger, strife, irritation, injustice, or other disharmonies, and with it we harm both ourselves and others to whom we spread its essence through sound, breath, touch, etc. When an animal is killed, it generates strong imperil in its flesh by fear and pain, and when people eat that flesh they consume the black astral-etheric crystals and accumulate them. *This is one of the main esoteric reason for vegetarianism.* Imperil and cosmic imperil or AEROPERIL accumulated in human populated areas and settles into the valleys and cities. That is why cities are poisonous, and disciples must retreat from time to time into pure nature, near the sea (which purifies imperil), or high on hills and mountains, where the psychic environment is fairly free of imperil. That is also why as disciples become more sensitive and attuned, they MUST do PURIFICATION PRACTICES and AURIC CLEANSINGS using sound-light practices and Temple Soap.

KAMA

Lust, desire; personal emotional attachments. Purified becomes aspiration motivating spiritual self-evolution.

KAMA LOKA

Astral world where, after physical death, the human "soul," mind, or consciousness is purified by testing—Purgatory. Also place of "hungry ghosts" of Tibet—humans who have died before their time, suicides, murder victims and other *caballi.* The purified elements of the Fifth Principle ascend out of Kama Loka into Devachan ("Heaven") with Sixth and Seventh Principles in cases of average spiritual achievement, but in lesser cases the Fifth Principle or Animal Soul is separated permanently from the higher principles and falls into the proctodernal regions of fiery decay, or Avitchi. One experiences a "second death" to either ascend or descend from Kama Loka.

LOKA

State of being, aeon, olam. The aeonic worlds are divided into five by the Tibetans according to the five classes of sentient beings: DEVAS,

MEN, ASURAS (elementals in human form), BEASTS (elementals in animal forms), DEVILS. Of these we can speak of Rupa-Devas (having form, as certain kinds of Dhyan Chohans), and the Arupa-Devas (having no form)—both kinds evolved from human beings. There are human "shells" or separated personalities containing the first four to five principles, Mara-Rupas or human "shells" doomed to annihilation in Avitchi, human ghosts containing two principles (astral shells). The RAKSHASAS are the sorcerer-adepts, many from ancient Atlantis, who form the Brotherhood of the Shadow or Dark Brotherhood. They have cheated nature and the "second death," managing to exist as adepts in the bodies of their first five principles, inhabiting the Astral and Mental planes as well as Physical-Etheric and even Physical. They live parasitic on the vital energy and emanations of others, holding the inverted consciousness of from preterodernal, infernal, and proctodernal states and infecting all nature and humanity with the poisons of maya and egoic consciousness. Their final destruction will come when our planet enters its OBSCURA-TION at the end of the Seventh Planetary Round, but Templars receive power to successfully checkmate and hold at bay even the most powerful of the Rakshasas ("Fallen Angels").

MONAD
The pure dyad of Sixth and Seventh Principles from which incarnate human life is projected and to which the Fifth Principle or Animal Soul must return with its store of spiritual treasure if the reflected world is to be joined to the Divine World to create conditions for the Autogenes, Self-Born, Christed or Resurrected One to come into gestation as a Divine Individuality.

PRINCIPLES
The Seven Macrocosmic-Microcosmic Principles in Mankind. The first three are minor and lost with physical death, but absolutely necessary for development into incarnation:

- First Principle (the final one developed through devolution into incarnation): The Physical Body
- Second Principle: The Astral Body
- Third Principle: Prana
- Fourth Principle: Kama
- Fifth Principle: Manas—seat of the Higher Self or Egoic Lotus which must evolve through purifications so that it can be united to Sixth and Seventh Principles to achieve permanence as a self-aware Individuality with continuity of consciousness.
- Sixth Principle: Buddhi
- Seventh Principle: Atma

PROCTODERNAL, INFERNAL, AND PRETERODERNAL FORCES

The infernal or lowest of the seven subplanes of Astral and Mental planes is itself divided into seven sub-subplanes which have a tripartite division (the SEVEN is an elaboration of the THREE, which is an elaboration of the ONE). In the simpler tripartite division, the upper infernal forces are called the PRETERODERNAL FORCES. The beings of this level do not know they are of the lower astral or mental, and they seek intercourse with humans through mediums in order to guide them spiritually. But their work ultimately turns negative because of their pride and ignorance. This is the source of most "channeled" teachers of New Age psychics. The middle region of the tripartite division contains the INFERNAL FORCES as normally recognized, and it is into this region preterodernal beings may eventually fall if on the devolutionary path to Avitchi. This is the place of Western demons, devils, fiends, vampires, animal-human beasts, etc. The lowest of the Mental and Astral sub-subplane regions is that of the PROCTODERNAL FORCES. These no longer have human or animal form, but exist as the foulest of energies, motions, and currents that constitute the Gateway to Avitchi. It is also known as

Geheena, The Pit, the cosmic garbage heap. It is a vortex of forces from which IMPERIL is formulated and moved into our plane of reality.

RUPA
Form of any kind, whether physical or not.

RECOMMENDED BOOKS BY OTHER AUTHORS

(available at westernesotericbooks.com)

Achad, F. (1923). *The chalice of ecstasy*. Illinois: Yogi Publication Society.

Aivanhov, O. (1992). *A new earth*. USA: Provesta.

Aivanhov, O. (1989). *The book of Divine magic*. California: Provesta, USA.

Amis, R. (1995). *A different Christianity*. New York: SUNY.

Atteshlis, S. (1994). *The esoteric practice: Christian meditations and exercises*. Cyprus: The Stoa Series.

Bailey, A. (1979). *Discipleship in the new age*. New York: Lucis Publishing Co.

Bailey, A. (1971). *Education in the new age*. New York: Lucis Publishing Co.

Bailey, A. (1982). *Glamour: A world problem*. New York: Lucis Publishing Co.

Bailey, A. (1979). *Letters on occult meditation*. New York: Lucis Publishing Co.

Bailey, A. (1971). *Ponder on this*. New York: Lucis Publishing Co.

Bailey, A. *The science of meditation*. Pamphlet. New York: Arcane School.

Boyer, G. & Keizer, L. (1994). *Collected writings of Richard Duc de Palatine*. California: Privately Published.

Corinne, H. (1986). *Mysteries of the holy grail*. California: New Age Bible and Philosophy Center.

Ellwood, R. (1997). *The cross and the grail: Esoteric Christianity for the 21stcentury*. Illinois: Quest Books.

Faivre, A. (1994). *Access to Western Esotericism*. New York: State University of New York Press.

Gardner, K. (1998). *Music as medicine: The art and science of healing with sound*. Audio-program. Colorado: Sounds True.

Gardner, K. (1990). *Sounding the inner landscape*. Maine: Caduceus Publications.

Kaplan, A. (1991). *Inner Space*. New York: Moznaim Publishing.

Kaplan, A. (1985). *Jewish meditation*. New York: Shoken Books, Inc.

Kaplan, A. (1978). *Meditation and the Bible*. Maine: Samuel Weiser.

Kaplan, A. (1995). *Meditation and Kabbalah*. London: Jason Aronson.

Keizer, L. (1986). *Esoteric principles of song and chant*. California: Privately Published.

Keizer, L. (1999). *Harmonic intoning and chanting: Instruction in vocal technique and esoteric principles of chakra attunement*. California: Home Temple Press.

Keizer, L. *Introduction to meditation*. California: Privately Published.

Keizer, L. (1998). *The authentic Jesus: A guide to Aramaic idioms, recent research, and the original message of Jesus Christ*. California: Privately Published.

Markides. K. (1985). *The Magus of Strovolos*. New York: Penguin Books.

Roerich, H. (1980). *AUM*. New York: Agni Yoga Society.

Roerich, H. (1977). *Hierarchy*. New York: Agni Yoga Society.

Roerich, H. (1981). *Letters of Helena Roerich, Volume 2*. New York: Agni Yoga Society.

Saraydarian, T. (1990). *Ageless wisdom.* California: T.S.G. Publishing.

Saraydarian, T. (1973). *Cosmos in man.* Arizona: Aquarian Educational Group.

Saraydarian, T. (1975). *Hierarchy and the plan.* Arizona: Aquarian Educational Group.

Saraydarian, T. (1991). *The flame of the heart.* California: TSG Publishing Foundation.

Saraydarian, T. (1981). *The psyche and psychism,* volume two. Arizona: Aquarian Educational Group.

Saraydarian, T. (1971). *The science of meditation.* California: Aquarian Educational Group.

Saraydarian, T. (1977). *Triangles of fire.* California: Aquarian Educational Group.

Temple. (1948). *Teachings of the temple.* California: The Temple of the People.

Yarker, J. (1909). *The arcane schools.* Privately Republished.

Index

W

About the Authors

The +GM+ does not disclose his name to the general public. He has taken the most advanced spiritual initiations of several Western and Eastern inner schools and holds lineages and charters for many of them. He serves as Grailmaster of the Temple of the Holy Grail (T:.H:.G:.) and Grand Master of the Pansophic Rites of Freemasonry. With his wife, he is also founding Bishop and Director of the Home Temple, which provides unique distance-learning training and ordination in Apostolic Priesthood. The +GM+ was one of the scholars who translated, edited, and interpreted parts of the historic Nag Hamadi Coptic Gnostic library. He has been a member of the religion faculty at the University of California and currently teaches Religious Studies for the U.C. Santa Cruz Extension. Among his numerous writings are The Authentic Jesus and The Simple Word of the Master Jesus.

Rev. Timothy A. Storlie, MS, MSW serves as President and Spiritual Director of the Interfaith Institute and Theological Seminary. An Independent Apostolic Bishop and ordained Interfaith Minister, Rev. Storlie has completed over 20 years of study and practice in various expressions of the Western Esoteric Traditions. Professionally, he serves as a Licensed Mental Health Counselor and Medical Social Worker.

16729705R00141

Made in the USA
Lexington, KY
08 August 2012